ON
CANADIAN
POETRY

E. K. BROWN

The Tecumseh Press — Ottawa
1973

Reprinted with the permission of McGraw-Hill Ryerson
Press and Mrs. E. K. Brown.

First Published, September 25, 1943

Designed by Thoreau MacDonald

This printing, from the revised edition, 1944

ISBN 0-919662-50-1

Printed and Bound in Canada
by Hunter-Rose Ltd., Toronto.

To
Arthur
who set me the task
and to
Peggy
who held me to it

Preface

THIS is less an historical enquiry than a critical essay. I have tried to answer three questions important to the reader of modern Canadian poetry, questions he must answer if his judgment is to have perspective. The first question is: What are the peculiar difficulties which have weighed upon the Canadian writer? In the first section (parts of which are reprinted from *Poetry*, April, 1941, and from *Canadian Literature Today*, University of Toronto Press, 1938) I have described and estimated these difficulties as I see them. The second question is: What Canadian poetry remains alive and, in some degree at least, formative? In the second section I have given a brief history of our poetry from the point of view set by this question. The final question is: How have the masters of our poetry achieved their success and what are the kinds of success they have achieved? In the third section, writing of the three poets who seem to me pre-eminent, I have tried to answer this, the most taxing of the questions. I cannot hope that all will agree with my conception of the difficulties or with my choice of living poetry, or of pre-eminent masters; but I am convinced that if the reading of contemporary poetry is to be illuminated by the past course of Canadian poetry, as I am sure it can be, such attempts at critical judgments are necessary.

It is with cordial pleasure that I acknowledge a number of obligations. Dr. Duncan Campbell Scott and Professor E. J. Pratt have followed my project with sympathetic interest, and have answered my questions with kindness and insight. Mr. and Mrs. T. R. Loftus MacInnes allowed me to use the precious notebooks of Mrs. MacInnes's father,

Archibald Lampman. Sir Charles Roberts wrote to me a valuable account of the prospects for Canadian Literature as they appeared to him in 1880. To the staffs of the Parliamentary and municipal libraries at Ottawa I am indebted for many courtesies and privileges.

E. K. B.

Goldwin Smith Hall,
Ithaca, N.Y.
June, 1943.

PREFACE TO THE SECOND EDITION

THE opportunity to revise this essay has come within a year of its publication. In its outlines it remains the same, but a considerable number of passages have been modified, often because of illuminating criticism which has come to me either in the reviews or in private letters. To the first chapter I have added a brief passage on the role of national crisis in the development of a literature. The relevance and importance of the problem was pointed out to me in varying ways by Dr. Lorne Pierce and Mr. Henry Ferns. In the later pages of the second chapter I have taken account of the poetry published since my first edition went to press, notably of Mr. A. J. M. Smith's *News of the Phoenix* and Miss Dorothy Livesay's *Day and Night*. In the chapter on Archibald Lampman I have added passages inspired by his lecture "Two Canadian Poets" which was unknown to me a year ago, but which I have since made generally available in the *University of Toronto Quarterly* (July, 1944). I have appended a brief calendar of significant dates.

My admiration for the stream of French-Canadian poetry from Crémazie through Fréchette and Nelligan to

Choquette and Brien is profound. In restricting this
essay to the Canadian poetry in the English language I
have not thought it necessary to narrow the term "Canadian
poetry" by any of the clumsy hyphenations which have on
occasion been employed: convention has ratified the use
of the term "Canadian poetry" in English works to
denote the poetry written by Canadians in the English
language, as it has ratified the use of the term *poésie
canadienne* in French works to denote poetry written in
the other of our two great national idioms.

E. K. B.

Wieboldt Hall,
The University of Chicago,
August, 1944.

Contents

ON CANADIAN POETRY

CHAPTER ONE

The Problem of a Canadian Literature

I

TOWARDS the end of his life Matthew Arnold expressed his disapproval of a tendency in the United States to speak of an American literature. American authors should be conceived, he suggested, as making their individual contributions to the huge treasury of literature in the English language. It was wrong to deal with the Americans who made such contributions as if they formed a group apart, with a peculiar unity of its own. The reality of the unity among American writers is now so obvious as to be accepted by everyone who is not a crank. It has been demonstrated in histories, anthologies and critical studies, and not once but a hundred times, that to consider an American writer or a group of American writers as American is one of the most illuminating approaches one could make. There are, it need scarcely be said, other illuminating approaches: just as it would not be sufficient for the student of Carlyle to consider him solely in relation to his British predecessors, and contemporaries, so it would not be sufficient for the student of Emerson to consider him solely in relation to other Americans. But the study of Emerson against his American background is just as rewarding as the study of Carlyle against his British background. This is what is meant by saying that American literature is a useful concept, and the study of American literature an illuminating study. In expressing his disapproval of such a study Arnold was satisfied that he had reduced the idea to absurdity by pointing to an unbelievable future which would see histories of Canadian and Australian literature. "Imagine the face of Philip or Alexander at hearing of a Primer of Macedonian Literature! Are we to have a Primer of Canadian Literature, too, and a Primer of Australian?" I think the time has come when to doubt the value of the concept of a Canadian literature, or an Australian, is to be a crank: a beginning has been made towards demonstrating that among Canadian, and Australian, writers, as among Americans, there is a peculiar unity, a unity sufficiently important as to make the approach to Canadian or Australian writers as Canadians or Australians a sharply illuminating approach. As I said above, in speaking of American writers, the national approach is not adequate, it is not the only illuminating approach, but it is valuable, and it throws into relief significant aspects which would otherwise fail to attract the attention that is their due.

At the beginning of his *History of English Canadian Literature to Confederation* Professor R. P. Baker defines his scope when he says that "it is wiser to consider only those authors of Canadian descent who maintained their connection with their native country and those of European birth and education who became identified with its development." In accepting this definition I should like to develop it to a point where it will have greater precision. By Canadian literature I shall understand writing by those who having been born in Canada passed a considerable number of their best creative years in this country, and also writing by those who, wherever they may have been born, once arrived in Canada did important creative work and led much of their literary life among us. Although this definition continues to have an element of indefiniteness, it will, I believe, serve to cover every author who will come before us in the development of Canadian poetry. I should add that, like Professor Baker, I shall include among Canadian writers those who wrote in any of the British colonies which now form part of the Canadian confederation even if at the time when they wrote their place of residence was outside what was then described as Canada: the significance of this addition will be to include all the Maritime authors whose lives, or literary lives, had ended by the time that the Canadian Confederation came into existence.

II

There is a Canadian literature, often rising to effects of great beauty, but it has stirred little interest outside Canada. A few of our authors, a very few, have made for themselves a large and even enthusiastic audience in Britain or in the United States or in both. Among these the first in time was Thomas Chandler Haliburton, a Nova Scotian judge, who would not have relished the claim that he was a Canadian. A curious blend of the provincial and the imperialist, he ended his days in England, where long before he himself arrived his humorous sketches were widely read, so widely that Justin McCarthy has reported that for a time the sayings of his most ingenious creation, Sam Slick, were as well known as those of the more durably amusing Sam Weller. Haliburton's papers were also popular in the United States, and their dialectal humour and local colour have left a perceptible stamp upon New England writing. At the mid century, when Sam Slick was already a figure in English humour, *Saul*, a huge poetic drama by a Montreal poet, Charles Heavysege, had a passing vogue in Britain and in the United States, impressing Emerson and Hawthorne and inducing Coventry Patmore to describe it as "indubitably one of the most

remarkable English poems ever written out of Great
Britain." Its vogue was lasting enough for W. D. Lighthall, a Montreal poet of a later generation, to recall that
"it became the fashion among tourists to Montreal to buy
a copy of *Saul*." Today, along with Heavysege's other
works, his *Count Filippo* and his *Jephthah's Daughter*, it is
unknown within Canada and without. Even the songs and
sonnets of Heavysege are absent from recent Canadian
anthologies. At the turn of the century the animal stories
of C. G. D. Roberts extended the range of North American
writing in a direction it might naturally have been expected
to take with equal success somewhat sooner—the imaginative presentation of the forms of wild life characteristic of
this continent in their relationship to the frontiers of
settlement. These tales, simple and at times powerful,
continue to hold a high place in the rather isolated and
minor kind of literature to which they belong; but there is
no doubt that in our time they are more talked of than
opened except by youthful readers. There is little need for
comment upon the writings of a handful of Canadians who
at about this same time began to make their huge and
ephemeral reputations as best-selling writers. Gilbert
Parker soon left Canada to establish himself in Britain, and
it is to English literature, to that group of British novelists
who followed in the wake of Stevenson's romantic fiction,
that his work belongs. Preëminent among the others,
Ralph Connor, L. M. Montgomery and Robert Service,
continued to live in Canada, the first two until they died,
Service till middle age. They were all more or less aggres-
sively unliterary; and their only significance for our inquiry
is the proof they offered that for the author who was
satisfied to truckle to mediocre taste, living in Canada and
writing about Canadian subjects, was perfectly compatible
with making an abundant living by one's pen. The lesson
they taught has not been forgotten: fortunately it has not
been widely effective.

More recently Canadian work of value comparable with
that of Haliburton's sketches and Roberts's animal tales
has become known outside the country.   There were the
humorous papers of Stephen Leacock, the best of which
have delighted not only Americans and Englishmen, and
the peoples of other parts of the British Commonwealth,
but also some Europeans.   I can remember hearing
M. André Maurois read to a group of students at the
Sorbonne the charming study called "Boarding House
Geometry"; and I never heard merrier laughter in Paris.
The endless Jalna chronicles of Miss Mazo de la Roche
maintain a large audience in Britain, and a sizable one in
the United States; and in a more restricted group in the
latter country the short stories and, to a less degree, the
novels of Morley Callaghan are valued.   I think that I
have mentioned all the Canadians who have acquired
considerable popularity or reputation as imaginative
authors, either in the United States or in Great Britain.
To the reader outside Canada such works as have been
mentioned have not been important as reflections of phases
in a national culture; the interest in the work has not spread
to become an interest in the movements and the traditions
in the national life from which the work emerged.   Canadian books may occasionally have had a mild impact outside
Canada; Canadian literature has had none.

III

Even within the national borders the impact of
Canadian books and of Canadian literature has been
relatively superficial.   The almost feverish concern with
its growth on the part of a small minority is no substitute
for eager general sympathy or excitement.   To one who
takes careful account of the difficulties which have steadily

beset its growth its survival as something interesting and
important seems a miracle.

Some of these difficulties, those of an economic kind,
may be easily and briefly stated. Economically the situation of our literature is, and always has been, unsound.
No writer can live by the Canadian sales of his books.
The president of one of our most active publishing com-
panies, the late Hugh Eayrs, estimated that over a period
of many years his profit on the sales of Canadian books was
one per cent.; and I should be surprised to learn that any
other Canadian publisher could tell a much more cheerful
tale, unless, of course, the production of text-books was the
staple of his firm's business. Text-books make money in
any country. In general the Canadian market for books
is a thin one, for a variety of important reasons. The
Canadian population is in the main a fringe along the
American border: nine out of ten Canadians live within
two hundred miles of it, more than half within a hundred
miles. The one important publishing centre is Toronto;
and a bookseller in Vancouver, Winnipeg or Halifax must
feel reasonably sure that a book will be bought before he
orders a number of copies which must be transported across
thousands of miles. Books like *Gone with the Wind* and
The White Cliffs—to keep to recent successes—he will
order in quantity with confidence; but the distinguished
work, the experimental novel, the collection of austere verse,
the volume of strenuous criticism, is for him a luxury.
The population of Canada is less than that of the State of
New York; if our population were confined within an area
of the same size the problem of distributing books would be
soluble. Even if our fewer than twelve million people
were confined within the huge triangle whose points are
Montreal, North Bay and Windsor—enclosing an area
comparable with that of the region of New England—the
problem might be soluble. But it is hard to see how the
cultivated minority is to be served when its centres are

separated by hundreds if not thousands of miles in which
not a single creditable bookstore exists.

Of the fewer than twelve million Canadians who are
strung along the American border in a long thin fringe,
almost a third are French-speaking. These read little if at
all in any language except French, apart from a small,
highly conservative minority which studies the classics
and scholastic philosophy, and a rather larger minority
which keeps abreast of books in English that treat of
political and economic subjects. In French Canada the
sense of cultural nationality is much stronger than in
English Canada, but the nationality is French Canadian,
not Canadian *tout court*. French Canada is almost without
curiosity about the literature and culture of English
Canada; most cultivated French Canadians do not know
even the names of the significant English Canadian creative
writers, whether of the past or of the present. Occasionally
an important Canadian book is translated from the original
into the other official language; but it is much more likely
that the work of a French Canadian will be translated into
English than that the work of an English Canadian will be
translated into French. Louis Hémon was a *Français de
France*, but it was because *Maria Chapdelaine* dealt with
French Canada that a distinguished Ontario lawyer translated the novel into English, making one of the most
beautiful versions of our time. W. H. Blake's translation
of Hémon's book is a masterpiece in its own right; no
French Canadian has as yet laboured with such loving
skill to translate any book that deals with English Canada.
A symbol of the fissure in our cultural life is to be found in
the definition of sections in The Royal Society of Canada.
Three sections are assigned to the sciences, one to mathe-
matics, physics and chemistry, another to the biological
sciences, and the third to geology and allied subjects; in
these sections French and English fellows sit side by side.
But in the two sections assigned to the humanities the

French and English fellows are severely separate: in each the subjects run the impossible gamut from the classics to anthropology. It is not too much to say that the maximum Canadian audience that an English Canadian imaginative author can hope for is fewer than eight million people.

To write in the English language is to incur the competition of the best authors of Britain and of the United States. Every Canadian publisher acts as agent for American and British houses; and it is as an agent that he does the larger and by far the more lucrative part of his business. Every Canadian reviewer devotes a large part of his sadly limited space to comment on British or American books. Every Canadian reader devotes a large part of the time and money that he can allow for books to those which come from Britain and the United States. Some angry critics have contrasted the plight of Canadian literature with the eager interest that Norwegians take in the work of their own authors. It is obvious that the accident by which Canadians speak and read one of the main literary languages of the world is a reason why they are less likely to read native books than a Norwegian is, speaking and reading a language peculiar to his own country.

Our great distances, the presence among us of a large minority which is prevailingly indifferent to the currents of culture that run among the majority, the accident of our common speech with Britain and the United States—here are three facts with enormous economic importance for literature. The sum of their effect is the exceedingly thin market for the author who depends on Canadian sales. Unless an author gives all or most of his time to writing for popular magazines he can make very little indeed; and even the resort of the popular magazines is a precarious solution. There are few of these—they, too, are affected by the factors that have been mentioned. They are in almost ruinous competition with American magazines, they cannot pay very much, they print a good deal written outside

Canada, and they live so dangerous an existence they commonly defer slavishly to the standards of their average readers.

The serious Canadian writer has a choice among three modes of combining the pursuit of literature with success in keeping alive and fed. He may emigrate: that was the solution of Bliss Carman, and many have followed in his train. He may earn his living by some non-literary pursuit: that was the solution of Archibald Lampman, and it has been widely followed. He may while continuing to reside in Canada become, economically at least, a member of another nation and civilization: that is the solution of Mr. Morley Callaghan. Each of these solutions is open to danger and objection.

The author who emigrates becomes an almost complete loss to our literature. It is probable that in the end, like Henry James or Joseph Conrad or Mr. T. S. Eliot, he will take out papers of citizenship in the country where he has found his economic security and to which he has transferred his spiritual allegiance. If he goes to Britain, the choice will not arise in this form, but he will be at best simply a citizen of the Empire ceasing to be an authentic Canadian. No one thinks of Grant Allen as a Canadian author nor did he so consider himself though he was born in Ontario. How the creative powers of a writer are affected by expatriation is much too vast a problem to receive adequate consideration here. Only this I should like to say: the expatriate will find it more and more difficult to deal vigorously and vividly with the life of the country he has left. Joseph Conrad did not write about Poland. When towards the end of his career Henry James read some of the early tales of Edith Wharton, before he had come to know her, he urged that she should be tethered in her own New York backyard. His own experience persuaded him that exile disqualified one from treating the life of one's own country without admitting one to the centre of the life in the country to which one had fled. If one compares the later novels of Edith Wharton, written after she had lost contact with New York, with the earlier ones which rose out of strong impacts that New York made upon her sensibilities, it is immediately evident that the colours and shapes are less vivid and definite, and that the works of her elder years are less significant. I should argue that Bliss Carman, our most notable exile, suffered a grave loss by passing his middle years in the United States, that he did not become an American writer, but merely a *déraciné*, a nomad in his imaginary and not very rich kingdom of vagabondia.

People often ask why an author cannot satisfy himself with the solution of Archibald Lampman. Lampman, after graduating from Trinity College, Toronto, entered the employ of the federal government as a clerk in the Dominion Post Office at Ottawa. Why, people inquire, cannot a writer earn his living as a clerk, or a teacher, or a lighthouse keeper and devote his leisure to literature? The answer to this question must be an appeal to experience. One of our most gifted novelists, Mr. Philip Child, once remarked to me that a writer must be the obsequious servant of his demon, must rush to write when the demon stirs, and let other things fall where they may. If you fob off the demon with an excuse, telling him to wait till you can leave the office, he will sulk, his visits will become rarer and finally he will not return at all. Temperaments differ; and some writers may, like Anthony Trollope, give fixed hours to authorship and the rest of the day to business and pleasure. Even the Trollopes of this world would prefer to be free from their unliterary employments, since it is not to manage a post-office that a Trollope came into this world. Temperaments less phlegmatic than Trollope's find even the mild yoke of the post-office too heavy for them. Lampman did. He had easy hours, from ten to four-thirty, work which did not exhaust, and long holidays; but he was irked

by his employment and made desperate and always
unsuccessful efforts to escape from it.   One has only to read
his letters to realize that he believed that his task-work
was fatal to his full development, and one has only to read
his poems to believe that there was something in Lampman
that never did come to full fruition, something that would
have led to deeper and wiser poetry than he did write except
in snatches.   It appears to me so obvious as to require no
argument that whatever success a particular writer may
have had in combining the practice of his art with the
business of earning a living by work which is remote from
letters, the notion that a whole literature can develop out
of the happy employment of the odd moments of rather
busy men is an unrealistic notion, and one that shows an
alarming ignorance of the process by which great works are
normally written.   I suggest that the richness of Canadian
poetry in the lyric and its poverty in longer and more
complicated pieces, in epic, or dramatic composition, is
related to the need of Canadians to be something else than
writers in most of their time through their best creative
years.   Some of them have, like Matthew Arnold—also
as a poet the victim of his unliterary employment—left
unfinished their main poetic attempt.

There remains a third solution, Mr. Callaghan's
solution.   It is possible to write primarily for an American
or a British audience.   Most of Mr. Callaghan's novels and
shorter tales are about the city in which he lives, Toronto;
but it seems to me, and I speak as one who was born and
brought up in that city, that Mr. Callaghan's Toronto is
not an individualized city but simply a representative one.
I mean that in reading Mr. Callaghan one has the sense that
Toronto is being used not to bring out what will have the
most original flavour, but what will remind people who live
in Cleveland, or Detroit, or Buffalo, or any other city on
the Great Lakes, of the general quality of their own milieu.
If one compares Mr. Callaghan's Toronto with Mr. Farrell's

Chicago, the point becomes very plain. When I pass through Mr. Farrell's Chicago, that part of the South Side which has been deserted by the Irish to be seized by the Negroes, the memory of what he has written of a life which has ceased to exist becomes very moving. When I walk through the parts of Toronto that Mr. Callaghan has primarily dealt with, the poor areas towards the centre and a little to the north-west of the centre, or the dingy respectability of the near east end, it is only with an effort that I remember that he has written of them at all. It is a notable fact that never once in all his novels does he use the city's name. Just as Mr. Callaghan uses his Canadian setting for its interest for a larger North American audience, so Miss Mazo de la Roche sets her emphasis on those exceedingly rare aspects of rural Ontario life which would remind an English reader of his own countryside and the kind of life that goes on in it. In the work of both writers an alien audience has shaped the treatment of Canadian life. Whether this peculiarity has injured the novelist's art as art, whether the characters and the setting are less alive and moving than the characters and setting in, let us say, Mr. Farrell's novels or Arnold Bennett's is not the immediate question; but there is not a scrap of doubt that the methods of Mr. Callaghan and Miss de la Roche have interfered with their presentation of Canadian life in the terms most stimulating and informing to Canadian readers. One of the forces that can help a civilization to come of age is the presentation of its surfaces and depths in works of imagination in such a fashion that the reader says: "I now understand myself and my milieu with a fullness and a clearness greater than before." Many a Russian must have said so after reading *Fathers and Sons* or *War and Peace*. It is difficult to believe that a Canadian will say this or anything of the sort after reading the work of Miss de la Roche or Mr. Callaghan.

I should like to turn for a moment to the question

momentarily put aside, the question whether the solution adopted by such writers as Mr. Callaghan and Miss de la Roche is injurious to their art, whether it reduces the worth of their fiction for readers who are not Canadians, and not interested in the problems peculiar to Canada as the ideal Canadian reader must be. A great opportunity has been refused by Mr. Callaghan—the opportunity of drawing the peculiarities of Toronto in full vividness and force. This is a subject that no writer has yet treated. Most Canadians who are not born and bred in Toronto emphasize that there is a quality in the life of that city which is to them mysterious, and obnoxious. To make plain what that quality is, perhaps to satirize it as Mr. Marquand satirized something peculiar to Boston in *The Late George Apley*, perhaps to give it a sympathetic interpretation as Arnold Bennett interpreted the Five Towns in *The Old Wives' Tale*—here was a great theme calling aloud for imaginative treatment. Had Mr. Callaghan not been essentially a part of American civilization, it would have forced itself upon his perceptive and completely realistic mind. There is also something unique in the life of rural Ontario, something that no novelist has succeeded in catching, and Miss de la Roche has refused an opportunity perhaps no less golden than Toronto offers.

IV

The difficulties that have so far appeared, unlike as they are, all have economic roots. It is time to turn to the psychological factors, implied in much that has been said, against which the growth of a Canadian literature must struggle.

Among these the most obvious, the most discussed, although *not* the most potent, is the colonial spirit. Long ago Harvard's President Felton doubted that Canada would come to much since a colony was doomed to be second-rate. In a later generation an American who knew us much better than Felton and who wished us well, William Dean Howells, used almost the same language. In *Their Wedding Journey* he conducts his couple from Niagara Falls by way of Kingston and Montreal to the east coast, giving sharp little pictures of the Canadian towns; he concludes that in comparison with the free nation to which they belong this colony is second-rate in the very quality of its life. Just a year or so ago the Halifax novelist, Mr. Hugh MacLennan, gave to one of the colonially minded characters in *Barometer Rising* the same thought: "I've wasted a whole lifetime in this hole of a town. Everything in this country is second-rate. It always is in a colony." These are probably independent judgments. What do they mean? That a colony lacks the spiritual energy to rise above routine, and that it lacks this energy because it does not adequately believe in itself. It applies to what it has standards which are imported, and therefore artificial and distorting. It sets the great good place not in its present, nor in its past nor in its future, but somewhere outside its own borders, somewhere beyond its own possibilities.

The charge that English Canada is colonial in spirit is the most serious of all the many charges that French Canada brings against us. Speaking in the 1942 session of the Canadian House of Commons, Mr. Louis Saint Laurent, the leading French member of the government, illustrated what he meant by our colonialism when he cited an interchange that is supposed to have occurred within the last few years between the two living ex-prime ministers of Canada. One said to the other, on the eve of his departure to live in England: "I am glad to be going *home*," and the other replied: "How I envy you!" For these two men—if the interchange did occur—Canada was

not the great good place; and every French Canadian would
regard their sentiments as justifying his practice of referring
to us not as *Canadiens Anglais*, but merely as *Anglais*, or
when his blood is up, as *maudits Anglais!* Colonialism of
this kind is natural to emigrants. One can easily forgive
Sir Daniel Wilson, although he spent almost his entire
active career in Canada, for wishing to lie in Scottish
earth; and yet for a Canadian who knows what Scotland
is like in November it is an awe-inspiring thought that Sir
Daniel on one of our autumn days, full of the crashing
scarlet glories of the Canadian forests or the mellow radiance
of our Indian summers, wished to be amid the "sleety east
winds" of his native land. What is odd, and unsatisfactory,
is the perpetuation of this kind of colonialism in the
descendants of emigrants even to the third and fourth
generation. It is clear that those who are content with
this attitude will seek the best in literature, where they
seek the best in jam and toffee, from beyond the ocean.
That anything Canadian could be supremely good would
never enter their heads.

It is important to distinguish this attitude of pure
colonialism from another, which is steadily confused with
it by all French Canadians, and combined with it by a good
number of English Canadians. As the nineteenth century
drew on and the concept of empire in Britain herself assumed
a new colour, the Kipling colour, some Canadians spoke and
wrote of a Canada which would be a partner in the destinies
of a great undertaking in which Britain would not be the
master, but simply the senior partner. Charles Mair, our
first important political poet, expressed the view I have in
mind when he wrote, in 1888:

> First feel throughout the throbbing land
>   A nation's pulse, a nation's pride—
> The independent life—then stand
>   Erect, unbound, at Britain's side.

Another poet, Wilfred Campbell, coined an impressive phrase for Canada's destiny: Canada was to be a part of "Vaster Britain." "Stronger even than the so-called Canadian spirit," he wrote, "is the voice of Vaster Britain." It is unjust to speak of this version of the imperialist ideal as showing the "butler's mind": it contemplated not serving Britain, but sharing Britain's glories. The psychological source of this intoxicating imperialism was not perhaps so much loyalty to Britain, but rather discontent with the dimensions of the Canadian scene. Canada was at the close of the last century a poor country, mainly concerned with material problems, and steadily losing many of her people to the large, rich, exultant land to the south. Imperialism was a kind of beneficent magic which would cover our nakedness and feed our starving spirits. The imperialist dream still lingers, but it is only a dream, for the mode in which the empire has evolved has been centrifugal—away from the concept of imperial federation—and there is nothing sufficiently rich and various to which the loyalty the dream evokes can attach itself. In practice the imperialist has drifted unconsciously into a colonial attitude of mind.

As the idea of imperial federation receded—and it was an idea that we may well judge impractical since French Canada could never have shared it, nor the Dutch in South Africa, nor the Southern Irish—Canada entered upon a period in which thinking was extremely confused. I cannot attempt to provide here any account of the extraordinary political evolution of the Dominions within the past generation. But the confusion is obvious if one notes merely a few significant political facts. Canada has no distinct flag, and no single distinct anthem although Mr. Mackenzie King paused on the very brink of asserting the latter; the relations between Canadian Provinces and the federal government are subject to review in London; and the Judicial Committee of the Privy Council, also in

London, is our highest court. But Canada has her own ministers in foreign countries, makes treaties without reference to Britain, and declares, or refuses to declare, war by the instrument of her own Parliament. Is it any wonder that Canadian thinking about Canada is confused, that one set of clear-thinking men demand that we cease sending ministers and signing treaties and declaring war for ourselves, and that another set of clear-thinking men demand that we provide ourselves with a distinct flag and anthem and end the ingestion of the British Parliament and the British Privy Council in our affairs? The average English Canadian would still like to have it both ways and is irritated, or nonplussed, by the demand that he make a resolute choice; at heart he does not know whether Canada or the Empire is his supreme political value.

In the contemporary world autonomy is the most luxurious of privileges, one which this anxious country cannot now afford and will not be able to afford in any measurable future. It is not an unmixed good. Autonomy almost always breeds chauvinism, and usually brings as an immediate consequence an unwholesome delight in the local second-rate. Its advent opposes strong obstacles to international currents of art and thought. This is to be set firmly against the notion that out of autonomy all good things soon issue. Still it must be appreciated just as clearly that dependence breeds a state of mind no less unwholesome, a state of mind in which great art is most unlikely to emerge or to be widely recognized if it did. A great art is fostered by artists and audience possessing in common a passionate and peculiar interest in the kind of life that exists in the country where they live. If this interest exists in the artist he will try to give it adequate expression; if it exists in the audience they will be alert for any imaginative work which expresses it from a new angle and with a new clearness. From what was said a moment ago it will be obvious that in a colonial or semi-colonial community neither artist nor audience will have the passionate and peculiar interest in their immediate surroundings that is required. Canada is a state in which such an interest exists only among a few. I have pointed out how Mr. Callaghan and Miss de la Roche have written as they could not have written if they had possessed such interest. It is the same with Canadian readers. A novel which presents the farms of the prairie, or the industrial towns of south-western Ontario, or the fishing villages in the Maritime Provinces will arouse no more interest in the general reader than a novel which is set in Surrey or in the suburbs of Chicago. Canadian undergraduates are much less likely than Americans to write stories about their immediate environment: their fancies take them to night-clubs in Vienna (rather than Montreal), islands in the South Seas (rather than the St. Lawrence), foggy nights in London (rather than Halifax). It is almost impossible to persuade Canadians that an imaginative representation of the group in which they live could clarify for the reader his own nature and those of his associates. To the typical Canadian reader such a notion is arty folly. I give this as a fact; and I offer as a partial interpretation, at least, that most Canadians continue to be culturally colonial, that they set their great good place somewhere beyond their own borders.

Somewhere beyond their borders—not necessarily beyond the seas. Canada is colonial not only in its attitude towards Britain, but often in its attitude toward the United States. It is true that the imprint of a London publisher, or of a British university press is a more impressive guarantee of a book or an author than any Canadian sponsorship, even a Governor-General's. When the late Lord Tweedsmuir remarked that a Canadian's first loyalty should be towards Canada (rather than towards Britain or towards the empire) it was believed in some circles, and these not the least cultivated, that he had been guilty, as one journalist phrased it in cynical fun, of "disloyalty towards himself." It was inevitable that a Scottish man of letters should think in such terms, Scotland being almost wholly free from the spirit of colonialism. Pleas that we should seek to free ourselves from our colonial feelings towards Britain are met with cries of "ingrate!" or "traitor!" There can, of course, be no question of such open and violent objection against efforts to free us from a colonial attitude towards the United States. Our colonialism in relation to the United States is unavowed, but it is deep. The praise of a couple of New York reviewers will outweigh the unanimous enthusiasm of Canadian journals from coast to coast. There is every reason to suppose that as Canadian feeling becomes more and more friendly towards the United States, as it has done during the past quarter century, our cultural dependence on the Americans will grow. If it does, our literature may be expected to become emphatically regionalist; of the dangers of regionalism something will be said a little later.

One consequence of our colonial or dominion status, and of our growing dependence on the United States and growing sense of security in American power, claims special note. Taking stock of our literature in 1891, and thinking in particular of the lack of national feeling or thought in it, Archibald Lampman wrote: "The time has not come for the production of any genuine national song. It is when the passion and enthusiasm of an entire people, carried away by the excitement of some great crisis, enters into the soul of one man specially gifted, that a great national poem or hymn is produced. We have yet to reach such an hour, and we may pray that it will not come too soon or too late." In the earlier years of the Confederation, when there was still some suspicion of the friendliness of the United States, Canadians felt that they had a strong defence in the force and prestige of England; and in later times the force and prestige of the

United States as well has been conceived as an assurance that Canada need not fear aggression. There has been no moment in our history comparable with what England knew on the eve of the Elizabethan efflorescence, when the Armada approached her shores, or at the height of the Romantic achievement, when Napoleon gathered his forces at Boulogne, or in the early summer of 1940, when the salvation of the country depended upon itself alone. Nor has Canada known an internal crisis at all comparable to the War between the States. It is probable that, as Lampman supposed, a national crisis of supreme intensity would call forth emotions of such a strength and purity as to issue in a significant expression in the arts. We are probably as far, or almost as far from such a crisis in 1944 as in 1891. The only tension to become impressively more dangerous is that between the French and the other strains in the Canadian population; and this tension, alarming as it is, stopped far short of crisis on the two occasions when it has become acute, 1917 and 1942. The essential orderliness and forbearance of the Canadian character allows one to believe that the inter-racial tension will not escape from control. On some other issue at some time not yet to be foreseen the passion and enthusiasm to which Lampman looked will surge up and there will ensue a fierce coming of emotional age. Our Whitman is in the future.

V

A more powerful obstacle at present to the growth of a great literature is the spirit of the frontier, or its afterglow. Most Canadians live at some distance from anything that could even in the loosest terms be known as a material frontier; but the standards which the frontier-life applied are still current, if disguised. Books are a luxury on the frontier; and writers are an anomaly. On the frontier a man is mainly judged by what he can do to bring his immediate environment quickly and visibly under the control of society. No nation is more practical than ours; admiration is readily stirred, even more readily than south of the border, by the man who can run a factory, or invent a gadget or save a life by surgical genius. This kind of admiration is a disguised form of the frontier's set of values. No such admiration goes out to any form of the aesthetic or contemplative life. The uneasiness in the presence of the contemplative or aesthetic is to be ascribed to the frontier feeling that these are luxuries which should not be sought at a time when there is a tacit contract that everyone should be doing his share in the common effort to build the material structure of a nation. That a poem or a statue or a metaphysic could contribute to the fabric of a nation is not believed. In a gathering of ruminative historians and economists, speaking their mind one evening in Winnipeg years before the war was imminent, the unanimous opinion was that a destroyer or two would do more than a whole corpus of literature to establish a Canadian nationality. The dissent of two students of literature was heard in awkward silence. If there were any belief in the national value of art or pure thought, the strong desire of the frontiersman that what is being built should eclipse all that was ever built before would make a milieu for art and thought that would at the root be propitious.

In a disguised form of frontier life what function can the arts hold? They are at best recreative. They may be alternatives to the hockey match, or the whiskey bottle, or the frivolous sexual adventure as means of clearing the mind from the worries of business and enabling it to go back to business refreshed. The arts' value as interpretation is lost in the exclusive emphasis on their value as diversion, and even their value as diversion is simplified to the lowest possible form—a work of art must divert strongly and completely. It must divert as a thriller or a smashing jest diverts, not as an elaborate and subtle romance or a complicated argument diverts. In a word, Canada is a nation where the best-seller is king, as it is on the frontier.

A third factor telling against the appreciation of art is our strong Puritanism. Every foreign observer notes with amazement, both in our French and in our English books, the avoidance of the themes that irk the Puritan, or the language that now irks him more. Canada has never produced a major man of letters whose work gave a violent shock to the sensibilities of Puritans. There was some worry about Carman, who had certain qualities of the *fin de siècle* poet, but how mildly he expressed his queer longings! Mr. Callaghan has fallen foul of the censors of morals in some of our more conservative cities, and even among those of his own Roman Catholic faith a novel as *Such Is My Beloved* has had an uneasy path; but how cautious in the description of sordor and how chastened in language he has always been! Imagination boggles at the vista of a Canadian Whitman, or Canadian Dos Passos. The prevailing literary standards demand a high degree of moral and social orthodoxy; and popular writers accept these standards without even such a rueful complaint as Thackeray made in warning that he could not draw his Pendennis as a full man, since no hero of an English novel intended for the general public had been drawn in full since Fielding went to his grave.

Even our Canadian Puritanism, however, has not been proof against the international currents of moral relaxation which have coursed so strongly during the past quarter century. In the poetry of those who are now approaching their fortieth year, there is a broad range of emotion, which does not stop short of carnality, and an equally broad range of speech for which nothing in the Canadian literary past gave a precedent. This poetry does not yet circulate at all widely, most of it is still locked away in periodicals read by few, and it is not possible to be sure whether it could even yet pass the moral test of the general reading public.

If Puritanism operated simply to restrain the arts within the bonds of moral orthodoxy, its effects, though regrettable, would be much less grave than they now are. Puritanism goes beyond the demand for severe morality: it disbelieves in the importance of art. It allows to the artist no function except watering down moral ideas of an orthodox kind into a solution attractive to minds not keen enough to study the ideas in more abstract presentations. At its most liberal Puritanism will tolerate, a little uneasily, the provision through the arts of an innocent passing amusement which is expected to leave no deep trace on character. To popularize orthodox morality and to provide light, clean fun—that is the very limit of what the arts can be allowed to do without alarming the Puritan mind. For the Puritan a life devoted to one of the arts is a life misused: the aesthetic life is not a form of the good life. That profane art, both for artist and for audience, may provide the contemplation of being, may offer an insight into the life of things, is for the Puritan mist and moonshine.

Puritanism is a dwindling force, and the time is not far off when it will no longer exercise its ruinous restraint upon the themes or language of a Canadian writer who is addressing the general public. Regionalism, another force which tells against the immediate growth of a national literature, cannot be expected to dwindle so fast. Canada is not an integrated whole. The Maritime Provinces recall the days—only seventy-five years in the past—when they were separate colonies; Nova Scotia, for instance, has re-established its colonial flag, dating from the eighteenth century and flying now from the Province House at Halifax; French Canada is a civilization apart; Ontario unconsciously accepts itself as the norm of Canadian life; the Prairie Provinces are steeped in their special vivid western past; and British Columbia has a strong sense of its pre-confederation life and of its continuing separate identity. Geography confirms the influence of history. Ontario is separated from the Maritime Provinces by the solid enclave of Quebec; between the populous southern part of Ontario and the prairies the Laurentian shield interposes another huge barrier; and this barrier is no stronger, if broader, than the Rocky Mountains create between the prairies and the coastal province of British Columbia. There is little doubt that the Fathers of Confederation, or the majority of the leaders among them, expected and planned for a much more unified whole than has so far come into being. In time of war the tendency to self-aggrandizement on the part of the Provinces is arrested, and even reversed; but there is ground for fearing that the return to peace will start it into vigorous being once more. Among most Canadians there is little eagerness to explore the varieties of Canadian life, little awareness how much variety exists, or what a peril that variety is, in time of crisis, to national unity. It may be that the next important stage of Canadian literature will be strongly particularist and regionalist: one remembers what a force regionalism was in American literature in the years after the Civil War.

Regionalist art may be expected to possess certain admirable virtues. One of these is accuracy, not merely accuracy of fact, but accuracy of tone; and throughout our literature there has been a disposition to force the note, to make life appear nobler or gayer or more intense than Canadian life really is in its typical expressions. It would help us towards cultural maturity if we had a set of novels, or sketches, or memoirs that described the life of Canadian towns and cities as it really is, works in which nothing would be presented that the author had not encountered in his own experience. It should also be acknowledged that a warm emotion for one's *petit pays* can lead to very charming art, as in Stephen Leacock's humorous transposition of an Ontario town in his *Sunshine Sketches*.   In the end, however, regionalist art will fail because it stresses the superficial and the peculiar at the expense, at least, if not to the exclusion, of the fundamental and universal.   The advent of regionalism may be welcomed with reservations as a stage through which it may be well for us to pass, as a discipline and a purgation.   But if we are to pass through it, the coming of great books will be delayed beyond the lifetime of anyone now living.

VI

What I have been attempting to suggest with as little heat or bitterness as possible is that in this country the plight of literature is a painful one.   People who dislike to face this truth—and most Canadians do—have many easy answers.   One is that Canadians have been so busy making a new world that it is harsh and unrealistic to expect that they might have written a large number of important books, read them with strong and general interest, and set a distinctive literary tone for their civilization.   To this answer one may retort by pointing to what had been achieved in the United States a century ago, calling the roll of the names of those Americans who had written works of the first order, of national and international importance, by 1844— Edwards, Franklin, Jefferson, Irving, Cooper, Poe, Hawthorne and Emerson.   In certain other ways the American environment up to 1844 was more hospitable to literature than ours has been up to the present time; but there can, I think, be no doubt that Americans were in the century and a half preceding 1844 just as busy building the material structure of a nation as we have ever been.   Another easy answer is often put in such terms as these: "If a Dickens begins to write in Canada we shall greet him with a cheer, we shall buy his books by the scores of thousands, get him appointed to the Senate of Canada, and request the Crown to give him an O.M. Meanwhile, don't bother us with your complaints. You can't point to a single man of anything approaching the calibre of Dickens who has written in this country. We have neglected no one of great importance. Wait till our Dickens comes along, and then we'll prove to you that we know how to honour a great writer." The line taken here depends on the belief that literature is an autonomous thing, a succession of single great men, each arising accidentally, each sufficient to himself. On this view you will get your great literature when you get your great men of letters, and meanwhile there is no problem worth discussing.

Thinking of this sort ignores a fundamental fact: that literature develops in close association with society. I should not deny that a single man of genius might emerge and express himself more or less fully in a society which was inhospitable to literature; but I find it significant that the most original of our poets, E. J. Pratt, has maintained:

The lonely brooding spirit, generating his own steam in silence and abstraction, is a rare spirit, if indeed he ever existed, and as far as one may gather from scientific discussions on the point, there is no biological analogy for this kind of incubation. Rather, the mountains come to birth out of the foothills, and the climbing lesser ranges. The occasional instance cited in literary history, of personal isolation ignores the context of spiritual companionship with books and causes and movements.

The ways of genius cannot be fully predicted; but the "occasional instance," the single man of genius, is not a literature and does not bring a literature into being. No doubt if a Browning or a Yeats were to write in Canada and to make himself felt in Canada, the effect on Canadian literature would be considerable. But the stimulus such a writer could give, great though it would be, and much as it may be wished for by all who hope for the growth of a great literature in this country, would be a passing stimulus, unless it were assisted by social conditions friendly to creative composition. A great literature is the flowering of a great society, a vital and adequate society. Here I must reluctantly take leave of the subject, for it is not in the province of a student of letters to say how a society becomes vital and adequate.

In the observations I have offered it will be thought by many Canadians that the note of pessimism, or at least of rigour, is too strong. On the side of hope and faith it should be said that the future of Canada is almost singularly incalculable: none of the factors that now tell so strongly against the growth of our literature is necessarily eternal, and many of them are likely to diminish in force. Every reflective Canadian must feel a mixture of disturbance and delight in our inability to foresee even the main stresses of the Canada that will exist a hundred years from now.

Chapter Two

The Development of Poetry in Canada

I

CANADIAN literature in the English language began on the Atlantic coast in the later years of the eighteenth century. For a few decades before the American Revolution Halifax had been the centre of a small colony, drawn in large part from the New England communities. One of the by-products of the American Revolution was the emigration of those who were resolved to remain British subjects and those whose loyalty to the new nation was questioned by their fellows. Many of these went to England, others preferred the West Indies or the wild and almost uninhabited lands to the north of the Great Lakes; a large number, over thirty thousand, came to what is now the maritime group of Canadian provinces, Nova Scotia, New Brunswick and Prince Edward Island. Their arrival gave a powerful and decisive impulse to the culture of these colonies in which Halifax was the focal point: it was essentially the culture of *exiles*, sometimes angry at their fate, sometimes hopeful that they might return before they died to their American homes. The religious verse of Henry Alline, the author of a large collection of hymns, might have come from Portland, or from some small town in the back country of New England; some of the satires might have been country cousins to the work of the Connecticut Wits if it were not for their scorn of the republicanism which had cost their authors their places in a settled society and sent them on their journey to a new, harsh and poor world; the little poem called "The Indian Names of Acadia" might have been Longfellow's. It is not too severe to say that scarcely any of the verse written in the Maritime Provinces up to Confederation has now more than historic interest. Here and there Alline, or Joseph Howe, or De Mille may achieve a line or even a stanza that is impressive; the mastery never endures throughout a whole piece. There is no Anne Bradstreet, no Edward Taylor, no Joel Barlow, no Freneau among the early poets of Nova Scotia or New Brunswick.

For the first poetry of lasting value one must look farther west. Kingston, on the shore of Lake Ontario, was also a loyalist town, the centre of a community which was predominantly loyalist, and which had built before the middle of the nineteenth century a social and economic structure which was a smaller, cheaper replica of communities in the eastern states from which its people had come. In Montreal, although there were loyalists, the English-speaking population was dominated by middle-class Scotsmen and Englishmen, to whose mode of life the loyalists partly conformed. It was a hundred years ago, as it is now, the financial capital of British North America: it was stamped with wealth and the preoccupation with big business; the grip of Puritanism was more relaxed than anywhere else in the British colonies; and imagination had an outlet in the almost unknown west from which came the furs which were the first base of Montreal's millions. The two chief figures in our pre-Confederation poetry are Charles Heavysege, a Montreal cabinet maker and journalist who had come out from Liverpool in middle age, and Charles Sangster, a Kingston journalist, born near that city, and returning to die there after spending his later years as a civil servant at Ottawa.

Sangster's life was perfectly representative of the

difficulties a poet must face in a pioneer community. It is clear that he never succeeded in finding a niche that suited him. As soon as he could he found work on a newspaper; and it was while he was harassed by a kind of activity that does not seem to have been compatible with his temperament—though the best a pioneer area offered—that he managed to bring out his two volumes of poetry, the first, *The St. Lawrence and the Saguenay and Other Poems*, in 1856 when he was thirty-four, and the second, *Hesperus and Other Poems and Lyrics*, four years later. Kingston was then one of the principal centres in Canada: it would probably be our capital city if it had not been so exposed to American attack; it was for a time the home of two men who in Sangster's lifetime were to be Prime Ministers of Canada, Alexander Mackenzie and Sir John A. Macdonald; it was the seat of an important university, and the source of much good journalism. The social environment was as propitious as an emphatically moral and bourgeois lyrist like Sangster could have found in Canada; nor was he unappreciated. In the year following Confederation he was appointed to a place in the Post Office in Ottawa, apparently as a recognition of his achievement in letters; and long before he had been asked, on occasion, to write official poetry. When the monument to General Isaac Brock was raised at Queenston in 1859, on the site where he was killed as his troops triumphantly resisted American invasion, it was Sangster who was charged with the memorial poem. His *Brock* is a fair sample of his powers as a patriotic poet. It begins:

> One voice, one people, one in heart,
>   And soul, and feeling, and desire!
>   Re-light the smouldering martial fire,
>   Sound the mute trumpet, strike the lyre,
>   The hero deed cannot expire,
>   The dead still play their part.

Raise high the monumental stone!
   A nation's fealty is theirs,
   And we are the rejoicing heirs,
   The honoured sons of sires whose cares
   We take upon us unawares,
     As freely as our own.

and in a more ambitious tone it ends:

Some souls are the Hesperides
   Heaven sends to guard the golden age,
   Illuming the historic page
   With records of their pilgrimage;
   True Martyr, Hero, Poet, Sage:
     And he was one of these.

Each in his lofty sphere sublime
   Sits crowned above the common throng,
   Wrestling with some Pythonic wrong,
   In prayer, in thunder, thought, or song;
   Briareus-limbed, they sweep along,
     The Typhons of the time.

This is Sangster when he has put on his formal singing robes: a little awkward, bent on doing his very best, and coming out of the ordeal with honour. It is not to write poetry of this sort that he came into the world.   His true note is much quieter.

It is the note of the best among the sonnets that he wrote in the woods near Orillia on the edge of Muskoka in the summer of 1859, when he found that:

My soul is dark and restless as the breeze
That leaps and dances over Couchiching.

or, in brighter moments:

I've almost grown a portion of this place;
I seem familiar with each mossy stone;
Even the nimble chipmunk passes on,
And looks but never scolds me.

It is the note of the purer stanzas in his confession of faith—
and doubt—"My Prayer," stanzas such as

> We walk in blindness and dark night
>   Through half our earthly way;
> Our clouds of weaknesses obscure
>   The glory of the day.

It is the note of his love-poetry, of such pieces as "Good
Night," with its admirable beginning:

> We never say, "Good Night";
> For our eager lips are fleeter
> Than the tongue, and a kiss is sweeter
>   Than parting words,
>   That cut like swords;
> So we always kiss Good Night.

Sangster has been rather carefully compared with Longfellow by Professor R. P. Baker, not with the cultivated
Longfellow who was free of the literature of all Europe, but
with the simple poet of "The Bridge" and "The Day is
Done"; and the comparison is suggestive. Sangster has
not, however, the soft melancholy that is like a patina on
Longfellow's more famous lyrics, and lends to them a
charm that is moving if in the end a little cloying. In all
his better work there is a firmness of temper that is more
like Whittier's; and it is this firmness that often enables
him to treat sentimental subjects without risking senti-
mentality. Related to this firmness, and perhaps deriving
from it, is a reluctance—perhaps it was an incapacity—to
express strong emotion. Sangster's guard is almost always
up: writing among and for a people whose reserve is almost
stern, he has his audience in view and records his experiences
and aspirations with caution. It is here, rather than in his
uncertain sense of language, that his chief defect as a lyric
poet lies, and it is a characteristic defect of art in a community where art is a stranger. It is easy to understand

his silence for the almost forty years of life that remained to him after the appearance of the *Hesperus* volume, easy to understand how he intended and planned a third collection and how he never came to publish it.   In commenting on his first poems a reviewer remarked: "A Canadian Poet, whose poems are far above mediocrity—whose songs are of Canada—her mountains, maidens, manners, morals, lakes, rivers, valleys, seasons, woods, forests, and aborigines, her faith and hope, merits encouragement.   Will he get it?" The answer is not a simple one.   Sangster received a great deal of encouragement, it will be clear; but he did not have around him that atmosphere of eager sympathy with poetry that is the most precious kind of encouragement, without which all other encouragement is a little artificial and in the end insufficient.

Sangster wrote for his fellow-Canadians, and about them and with a Canadian or, at the widest, a North American range of attitude.   Heavysege wrote for the world and for himself, of subjects entirely unconnected with Canada or North America—even his natural imagery is scarcely ever Canadian—and with a range of feeling that recalled the Byronic afterglow that was alive in the England from which he emigrated.

He was born in Liverpool; in 1853, when he came to Canada, he was thirty-seven, and already the author of a volume of poetry.   In Montreal, supporting a large family, he at first followed his trade as a cabinet-maker, and wrote, or it may be simply completed, his dramatic trilogy, *Saul*. The reception of this heartened him; it was admired by Emerson and Longfellow, Hawthorne and Patmore; it was called the greatest dramatic poem since the time of Shakespeare; it was called perhaps the greatest poem in the English language composed outside of Great Britain.   In middle age Heavysege left his bench to become a reporter, and he was not a successful reporter.   He appears to have been arrogant and exacting; to have hated his environment; and to have retired within himself. There is no doubt that in his elder years, at least, he was profoundly unhappy, all too conscious of the gap between the language that was used about his poetry and the mean way he earned his bread. At least one more notable work came from him, the dramatic poem, *Jephthah's Daughter*, which appeared in 1865.

It is a long time since Heavysege was even a name for the general Canadian reader. None of his pieces has even the slight popularity one might claim for Sangster's "Brock"; of them all perhaps the most familiar is the little poem:

> Open, my heart, thy ruddy valves;
> It is thy master calls,
> Let me go down, and curious trace
> Thy labyrinthine halls.
> Open, O heart, and let me view
> The secrets of thy den;
> Myself unto myself now show
> With introspective ken.
> Expose thyself, thou covered nest
> Of passions, and be seen;
> Stir up thy brood, that in unrest
> Are ever piping keen.
> Ah! what a motley multitude,
> Magnanimous and mean.

If one can pass quickly by the quaint and now absurd phrase that closes the first line, the poem can be impressive. It has a richer volume than anything that Sangster ever wrote; it is organ music to Sangster's little violin. It evokes memories of Scott and Byron and Moore, and is not unworthy to be set with their songs. It has the intensity of the popular romantics, an intensity that our poetry has all too often lacked even in its finest expressions.

Again and again Heavysege strikes this deep note, for instance at the close of "Twilight":

> the golden chime
> Of those great spheres that sound the years
> For the horologe of time;—
> Millenniums numberless they told,
> Millenniums a millionfold
> From the ancient hour of prime!

Here is a poet intoxicated with language, as his admired contemporary Poe was intoxicated; and one could wish that he had set himself to write with musical beauty of a fantastic world, as Poe wrote.

His preoccupation, however, was with drama, not with drama intended for the stage, but with the cabinet-drama of the romantics. *Saul* is cabinet-drama: it is closer to *Paradise Lost* than to a stage-play; it surprises one to learn that he prepared a text of *Saul* for a New York actress, a text which was never used and has long been lost. But recognition of the dramatic ineffectiveness of *Saul* has led many of Heavysege's modern detractors to deny him merits that he undoubtedly possesses. He has, for instance, considerable powers as a realist, even as a bitter humorist. It is impossible, I should think, for anyone to read *Saul* without being impressed by the dialogue he gives to the devils who play a large part in the tragedy. Line after line has the sharp poetic realism of Malzah's comment on seeing the body of Agag hacked in pieces:

> A pie;
> But made, methinks, lass, when the cook was angry.

The soldiers and minor officers have a dialogue scarcely less vivid and striking. One may pause on this remark made by one of the soldiers who is looking at the broken corpse of Agag:

Agag is now a ghost, and would not know
The carcass that three minutes ago contained him.
So felled it is, so lopped, so strewn on th' ground,
The bird, his soul, now would not know the tree
That it for forty years has sat and sung in.
He'll pipe no more.

The bird-image is plainly fanciful, in the manner of Scott
and Moore; but there is a vigorous temper in the lines, and,
apart from this image, poetic realism. With the higher
characters, Heavysege is not so steadily successful: like the
other nineteenth-century dramatists in the Elizabethan
tradition his approach to tragic character is insufficiently
realistic. Saul and David, Abner and Samuel are far from
breathing human beings: they always stamp about with
their buskins in proud view. Nor is his sense of tragic
action sounder: Saul is the prey of shifting passions, and if
at first we are moved by his impotence in their grip, when
the same see-saw has been repeated throughout the whole
trilogy, it merely wearies. A dramatic imagination seizing
on the tale might have graduated the crises, and given us a
feeling that Saul was in each act moving nearer to some
dread climax; Heavysege exploits the full resources of the
situation in the early acts of the first part.

Jephthah's Daughter is, strictly speaking, a narrative;
but it is essentially a dramatic poem, a succession of long
speeches tied together by brief passages describing the
settings. Its dramatic value is higher than *Saul's:* a single
tragic situation works itself out quickly and brings before
us the inner natures of at least two characters—Jephthah
and his daughter—who are more real to us than any of the
major figures in *Saul*, though less real than even such
romantic personages as Tennyson's Lancelot or Arnold's
Rustum. What is most attractive in *Jephthah's Daughter*
is the language, which has a richness of beauty that is rare
in *Saul*, a richness sometimes Miltonic, but more often
authentically nineteenth century. It was not till Carman

wrote "Low Tide on Grand Pré" that a Canadian would
again have the secret of such phrases as crowd from
Heavysege's pen, phrases like:

> . . . nor twilight dim,
> Sickening through shadows of mysterious eve,
> Die midst the starry watches of the night.

or

> The hill wolf howling on the neighbouring height,
> And bittern booming in the pool below.

Montreal was of all places in Canada the best for
Heavysege, but it was a meagre best. He wrote to an
American enthusiast in 1865: "Canada has not a large
cultivated class and what of such there is amongst us not
only misdoubts its own judgment, but has generally no
literary faith in sons of the soil, native or adopted." The
little community of merchants and financiers that was
English-speaking Montreal when he began to publish his
poems might take a certain pride in their appearance: this
was nevertheless not the kind of poetry that could really
matter to them—if any poetry could—and Heavysege had
no succession. W. D. Lighthall evokes Heavysege as "a
sombre shadow towering in the background of the group—a
man apart from the rest" of the early Canadian poets. He
is a significant example of a poet gifted in some ways almost
to the level of genius, and yet leaving no mark on the
development of a literature and a civilization.

II

Our poetry has had two main flowerings. The first
began in 1880 with the appearance of Charles G. D.
Roberts's first collection, *Orion*, and was already fading
soon after the turn of the century. Roberts was one of
four men born between 1860 and 1862 whose works were

the great performances in our first distinguished period. The others were Bliss Carman, a cousin of Roberts who announced himself in 1893 with *Low Tide on Grand Pré;* and Archibald Lampman and Duncan Campbell Scott, civil servants in Ottawa and close friends, whose first collections, *Among the Millet* and *The Magic House,* appeared in 1888 and 1893 respectively. Lampman died at the peak of his power in 1899; Carman lived on to 1929 and Roberts to 1943 at odds with the poetic ideals that arose after the war; Scott, although he has passed eighty, now and then publishes a notable poem.

But before we turn to the new poets, it will be well to say what needs to be said of two writers a little senior to them, although the appearance of their works in book form belongs to the period following the appearance of *Orion.*

George Frederick Cameron was a Nova Scotian by birth and upbringing. In 1869 when he was fifteen, the family moved to Boston, as many a Maritime family has done; and Cameron attended Boston College and subsequently joined a Boston law-firm; if he had remained in the United States his poetry would have no place in this survey; but for reasons that are not clear he decided in 1882 to move to Kingston, Ontario, where he attended Queen's University and was employed by a newspaper until his sudden death in 1885. His one collection, *Lyrics on Freedom, Love and Death,* was issued in 1887 by his brother, who promised that, if the book were well received, it would be followed by others, since it contained only about a quarter of the surviving verse. No later collection was undertaken, and nothing has been known of the character of Cameron's unpublished work.

Since Cameron is quite unlike any other Canadian poet, the loss of so much of his work is extremely unfortunate. He is the nearest to a citizen of the world among all our poets of the last century. Of his twenty-nine lyrics of freedom, thirteen have to do with Cuba, eight with Russia,

three with France, three with the United States, and one
with Ireland.   Only one of his political poems, and this a
weak piece not grouped with the lyrics of freedom, has a
Canadian theme.   The great political experiment of Canadian Confederation meant nothing to him, to whom the
American Civil War meant so much: his absence from
Canada in youth and early manhood does not account for
such indifference in one whose political preoccupation was
so strong.   How strong it was may be seen from his
attacks on Russian absolutism, attacks in which idea, feeling
and form have the imprint of Swinburne, as in these
representative lines:

> Hath he shown a contempt of the wrong?
>   Hath he shown a desire of the right?
> Hath he broken the strength of the strong,
>   Or supported the weak with his might,
> That to meet him and greet him ye throng?

This, a complaint against Boston's enthusiastic reception of
the Grand Duke Alexis Romanoff, is very good Swinburne
indeed.   In his Cuban poems the note is more Byronic, as
in this protest against Americans who were opposed to
Cuban efforts to achieve independence:

> Then gaze where Caribbean waves
>   Loll calm on desecrated sands;
>   Where Freedom cheers her weary bands:
> Where heroes dig heroic graves
>   With their own hero-hands.

Whether he writes in Byron's manner or Swinburne's,
Cameron is an accomplished rhetorical poet.   Above
rhetoric his political poetry never rises: there is nothing in
it like "The Isles of Greece," or "Siena."

The rhetorical manner is almost everywhere in his
poetry of love as well, recalling Byron and Moore.   Note
the orator's imagery in these lines:

> Mine?   Ah, alas! the barricade
>   That Mammon rears between us twain
> May not be overleaped, dear maid,
>   Though high hearts break with parting pain.
> The phantom passion must be laid
>   The harper taught another strain;
> The knee must seek another shrine,
>   For thou art not—*thou art not mine!*

It is significant that his most stirring treatment of love, in
the longest of his poems, "Ysolte," is in the manner of
"Maud," a rhetorical manner, with an intensity that is
nervous rather than authentically passionate.   How close
Cameron comes to Tennyson's manner in "Maud" appears
in these lines, breathing neurotic jealousy:

> The prowling fox has found his prey,—
>   An easy prey, an easy prize:
> So easy that some people say
>   It was a willing sacrifice.
> But I say neither yea nor nay,
>   Not having other people's eyes.

Is there, one may ask, no manner of Cameron's own? no
time when he is free of Byron and Swinburne and Tennyson,
and Shelley and Poe?

One of the chief powers in the poetry of Lampman and
his associates is their power in the handling of nature.
Before Cameron is left behind it will be well to note how
nature appears in his verse.   His treatment is well represented by these lines which form part of a poem sent back
to his sister Louise in Nova Scotia long after he had left the
colony and at a time when he yearned to revisit it,

> And pluck the flowers full-freighted with perfumes—
> With dew-drops sparkling, and by south winds fanned,—
> The flowers that gem the fields of our beloved land.

It is the nature of the English late-eighteenth century, of Gray and Goldsmith, conventional, generalized, supplying no picture, affording no surprise.   In Cameron a bird is a "silver-throated singer"; a fountain is "fringed with laurel"; the "placid wave" carries its calm foambell.   It is a rhetorician's nature, the nature of one whose mind has been on other things.   It is highly significant that the one nature-poem that his first season in Kingston suggested is a complaint against cold weather.   The new world about him gave no stimulus to his imagination; he was not curious to note and use its phenomena; he just felt that it was cold:

> What wonder we long for a breeze from the islands
> The beautiful islands and blest of the sea?—
> Vine-lands or pine-lands, lowlands or highlands,
> So they be *summer* lands nought care we!

Even the nature he dreams of is not particularized: anything will do, provided there is warmth.   It should be said that this poem was written, not in mid-February but in— November.

Interesting as Cameron's verse is, it must, I think, be admitted that nowhere does he fully satisfy, nowhere is he fully himself.   Set among the Canadian poets, he at first appears original because he is unlike the others in most respects; but when he is set among English and American poets of the age and of the age before, more particularly of the age before, he shows himself to be more like these than Lampman is, or Roberts.   The real originality, then, is not in Cameron but in his junior contemporaries.   We can now answer the question which was allowed to dangle some time past: has Cameron anywhere a manner of his own, is he anywhere notably and fully himself?   No. Perhaps had he lived—and it is to be remembered that he was only thirty when he died—such a manner might have developed.   Lampman, however, had his manner long before his development was complete, had it well before his thirtieth year.

Three years before Cameron's collection appeared at Kingston, a Toronto press produced *Old Spookses' Pass, Malcolm's Katie and Other Poems*, the work of a young woman who had been brought out from Ireland as a child when her parents emigrated to a village in Upper Canada, and who like Cameron was to die in her thirties. Isabella Valancy Crawford is the only Canadian woman poet of real importance in the last century; and her "Malcolm's Katie," a long narrative of backwoods life in primitive Ontario, is the best image a poet has given us of Canadian living in the years following Confederation. Malcolm Graem is a stern, silent, Scottish Canadian farmer, who has made his fields from the wilderness and every time he surveys them feels a rugged pride in property and accomplishment. His daughter Katie has the graces and the softer virtues that belong to a time of consolidation rather than back-breaking pioneer effort; but her love goes out to Max, a lumberman, who is a representative of a Canada more primitive than Katie's father's, a Canada where adventure is a deeper satisfaction than achievement, though achievement is not scorned. Clearly, in her way of presenting these personages, as in her style, Miss Crawford follows Tennyson, the Tennyson of the modern idylls; but in the style there is a density, at times a confused richness, which express a nature more nervous and ardent than Tennyson's.

Nowhere does her style appear to better advantage than in the description of nature, in such passages as these:

> At morn the sharp breath of the night arose
> From the wide prairies, in deep-struggling seas,
> In rolling breakers, bursting to the sky;
> In tumbling surfs, all yellow'd faintly thro'
> With the low sun; in mad conflicting crests,
> Voic'd with low thunder from the hairy throats
> Of the mist-buried herds. . . .

and

> In this shrill Moon the scouts of winter ran
> From the ice-belted north, and whistling shafts
> Struck maple and struck sumach, and a blaze
> Ran swift from leaf to leaf, from bough to bough;
> Till round the forest flashed a belt of flame,
> And inward lick'd its tongues of red and gold
> To the deep tranced inmost heart of all.

Both these passages come from the opening of the second part of "Malcolm's Katie," in which with more impressive result than anywhere else in her poetry Miss Crawford sought to convey the teeming vitality of nature. The density and confused richness in her manner, sometimes a fatal flaw, are here wholly appropriate: they do aid her in making the reader feel that nature is enormously and even terrifyingly alive. Not until Duncan Campbell Scott wrote his major nature poems was any other Canadian poet to rival Miss Crawford's adequacy in handling wild nature.

One of the most powerful forms in which Miss Crawford rendered nature was the combination of the dense and rich style with dialect which recalls the *Biglow Papers*. "Old Spookses' Pass" is written in this dialect, and there is much more than quaintness, there is a rare force of surprise and insight when the luxuriant and original imagery is set in humble dialect:

> An' the summer lightnin', quick an' red,
> Twistin' an' turnin' amid the stars,
>   Silent as snakes at play in the grass,
> An' plungin' their fangs in the bare old skulls
>   Uv' the mountains frownin' above the Pass;
> An' all so still that the leetle crick,
>   Twinklin' an' crinklin' from stone tew stone
> Grows louder an' louder   .   .   .

The passages that have been quoted suggest another of her powers, the power of fantastic imagination: indeed it is only because her imagination is wildly fantastic that those passages were written, that nature in her poetry is such a wild and exciting thing. In very trifling pieces this imagination appears to arrest the attention, in such comparisons as that of a girl's mobile eyes with "a woodbird's restless wing," a light laugh with "a zigzag butterfly," the flash of a jewel with the "silent song of sun and fire." The multitude of such images makes it unsafe to neglect even her most careless and unsatisfactory poems—and very much of her work is careless and unsatisfactory.

Often her poetry is unsatisfactory simply because it is carelessly conventional. She is very likely in her more relaxed passages to use a diction like Cameron's, in which fields are "gemmed" with flowers, a canoe has "polished sides" like a queen's, a mother's hair is "the holy silver of her noble head." There is a great deal of this sort of language in her poetry, and even in the middle of some of her intensely wrought passages it comes to mar the fine effect. In the second part of "Malcolm's Katie," where she is at her very best, she can speak of a tree as

> The mossy king of all the woody tribes

or of superb health as denoted by

> The rose of Plenty in the cheeks.

This carelessness, the sign of flagging energy and dubious taste, is perhaps, all in all, not so grievous a disappointment as some of the tricks played Miss Crawford by what is so often her strength—that very fantastic imagination some of whose flights have been recorded. Of these tricks I shall give but one example, a passage which has by some been highly admired:

> For love, once set within a lover's breast,
> Has its own sun, its own peculiar sky,
> *All one great daffodil*, on which do lie
> The sun, the moon, the stars all seen at once.

The utter lawless wildness of such a comparison is the penalty paid for the fantastic successes; and there is a great deal of such wildness, most of it far less acceptable than the lines quoted.

Some time ago it was said that in "Malcolm's Katie" Miss Crawford had given us the one poetic account of real Canadian living in the years following Confederation. She was able to do so because, despite her fantastic vein, she lived in the real Upper Canadian world of her time. She tells, for instance, of how into the edges of settlement came the business men:

> . . . smooth-coated men, with eager eyes,
> And talk'd of steamers on the cliff-bound lakes,
> And iron tracks across the prairie lands,
>
> And mills to crush the quartz of wealthy hills,
> And mills to saw the great wide-armed trees,
> And mills to grind the singing stream of grain. . . .

And over against this picture of the coming of a business civilization—how much there is in that one epithet, "smooth-coated"—in her best-known lyric, "The Song of the Axe," she celebrates the pioneer glory. She frames the song admirably, placing just before it the line:

> While the Great Worker brooded o'er His work

and after it this claim of Max's:

> My axe and I—we do immortal tasks—
> We build up nations—this my axe and I.

In the framework and in the tone of the song itself Miss Crawford comes nearer to Whitman than any of her contemporaries. The song itself is moving:

> Bite deep and wide, O Axe, the tree,
> What doth thy bold voice promise me?

> I promise thee all joyous things,
> That furnish forth the lives of kings!
>
> For ev'ry silver ringing blow
> Cities and palaces shall grow!
>
> Bite deep and wide, O Axe, the tree,
> Tell wider prophecies to me.
>
> When rust hath gnawed me deep and red,
> A nation strong shall lift his head!
>
> His crown the very Heav'ns shall smite,
> Æons shall build him in his might.
>
> Bite deep and wide, O Axe, the tree;
> Bright Seer, help on thy prophecy!

The old clothes are still there, but the new spirit is strong enough to shine through them, and to animate, as little of Sangster or Cameron can. Miss Crawford's vision was not strictly national, nor was Lampman's to be; but it was often fixed, as his was, on the real significance of the life immediately around her.

Something of the change brought to the style and feeling of our poetry by Lampman and the other poets born in the early 'sixties has been caught by James Cappon, who remarked in his monograph on Roberts:

> You can see the difference at once in the descriptive manner of the new poets, in the sensuous or mystical intensity of the verb and in the impressionistic delicacy of the epithet. The dawn no longer chills, it "bites"; it does not rise, it "leaps"; it is nothing so common as rosy, but has some elusive epithet attached to it, such as "inviolate" or "incommunicable." Darkness and night "reel"; the sea, the wind, the rain, the trees, all "sob"; the stillness of the woods is "expectant"; terms like "elemental," "largess," "lure," "sinister," slipped from their older and narrower usage into a wider power of suggestion. It was an evolution of a new poetic diction which reflected the more

intimate sense of the mystery of life and nature which was
arising in the new generation. A new and mystic form of
romanticism was coming into vogue.

The new richness, subtlety and mystery first found expression, although incompletely, in *Orion*.   Roberts was only
twenty when the book appeared, and many of the poems
where written when he was in his middle teens.   His subjects are Greek, and Greece is seen through the eyes of
Keats and Tennyson.   Roberts had received an excellent
classical education of the old sort at the Fredericton
Collegiate School and at the University of New Brunswick,
from which he had graduated a year before he brought out
the book.   His father and the headmaster of the school,
George R. Parkin, cared deeply for poetry, and the boy
had read widely, perceptively, formatively in the musical
and pictorial poetry of nineteenth-century England as well
as in the best books of the ancient world.   *Orion* is exactly
the kind of poem that a boy of Roberts's temper and
training might be expected to write, with its gentle, sensuous
pictures of women and nature, and its soft Tennysonian
music.   In his next collection, *In Divers Tones*, the qualities
of *Orion* are more impressively developed.   Here are the
vaguely beautiful pictures of women

> Perfectly fair like day, and crowned with hair
> The colour of nipt beech-leaves . . .
> Its soft thick coils about my throat and arms;
> Its colour like nipt beech-leaves, tawny brown,
> But in the sun a fountain of live gold

the vaguely beautiful idyllic landscape

> the grey-green dripping glens all bare,
> The drenched slopes open sunward

and the vaguely beautiful despair

> I have lived long and watched out many days,
> Yet have not learned that aught is sweet save life,
> Nor learned that life hath other end than death.

To the earlier Canadian poetry these first collections of
Roberts's owe nothing at all: with them Canadian poetry
begins anew.

What is important and lasting in the new beginning is
not the classical substance—Roberts himself was to
abandon this—but the quiet, sensuous manner, a manner
caught from the milder passages in Keats and Swinburne
and the early Tennyson.   This was the manner not only of
Roberts but of Carman and Lampman in much of their
best work.   Among the earliest of Lampman's notable
pieces, his "April," written in the spring of 1884, is pure
Keats:

> Pale season, watcher in unvexed suspense,
> Still priestess of the patient middle day,
> Betwixt mild March's humoured petulance
> And the warm wooing of green kirtled May,
> Maid month of sunny peace and sober gray,
> Weaver of flowers in sunward glades that ring
> With murmur of libation to the spring.

The mood of the "Ode to Autumn" is there as it is in so
many of the good pieces in Lampman's first collection.
Set these lines of his youth or any typical passage of the
early Carman, for instance,

> when athwart
> The dark a meteor's gloom unbars
> God's lyric of the April stars
> Above the autumn hills of dream

beside the poetry of Sangster or Heavysege and it leaps to
view that a subtler, more sensuous, more mystery-haunted

generation has come into being, a generation, too, that as Cappon says, had the language its preoccupations required.

A group of poets devoted to Keats and the early Tennyson, delighting in the subtleties of the senses and of words, full of a consciousness of the mystery in things, might turn to either of two subjects—nature or woman. The Canadian poets turned to nature.   It was the central theme of all the poets of the generation coming into view in the eighties and nineties.   They were concerned both with the surface of nature and with its central meaning.

Roberts is at his best when he deals with the surface. Nowhere in the whole range of his poetry is he better than in his pictures of rural New Brunswick and Nova Scotia. Where so much is of even goodness it is hard to know what to quote.   In his purely realistic manner he has never gone beyond some of the lines in "The Potato Harvest," lines like

A high bare field, brown from the plough, and borne
   Aslant from sunset; amber wastes of sky
   Washing the ridge; a clamour of crows that fly
In from the wide flats . . .

Roberts's sense for the word is not unerring, and usually in such purely simple verse as this he will sooner or later introduce unnecessary decoration in the desire to heighten his tone.   More typical of his good nature verse is a more elaborate and suggestive passage, such as this:

Out of the frost-white wood comes winnowing through
   No wing; no homely call or cry is heard.
   Even the hope of life seems far deferred.
The hard hills ache beneath their spectral hue.
A dove-grey cloud, tender as tears or dew,
   From one lone hearth exhaling, hangs unstirred,
   Like the poised ghost of some unnamed great bird
In the ineffable pallor of the blue.

Here he can be suggestive and mysterious while at the same time supplying a picture: the touch is harder and sharper than Lampman's or Carman's, but at a glance the passage is seen to be their kind of verse.

It would not be rewarding to linger over Roberts's interpretations of the inner meaning of nature. In this connection, though oddly Victorian in its mode of expression, Lampman's judgment may stand: "he has nothing to teach us beyond some new phases of the beauty of nature." Never a poet of philosophical ideas, he was not intimately affected by the intellectual anxieties that *The Origin of Species* and *The Descent of Man* had brought to the nature poets of Europe. God is in nature; and nature is good. Man is a part of nature; and has no quarrel with it. These simple, supremely optimistic notions, characteristic of Wordsworth's generation, and continuing on in the poetry of the American transcendentalists, are all that Roberts requires. It is typical of his temper and mind that these ideas are set forth obscurely, in a fashion which indeed prevents the rapid reader from deriving anything beyond a vague notion that all is mysteriously well. The heart of the universe, for instance, is described as

> the wisdom and the stillness
> Where thy consummations are.

His love poetry offers a special problem. Towards the end of the century Roberts left Canada, which was not again to be his home until after the First World War. In the atmosphere of New York City, in the company of *fin de siècle* spirits, he began to write a kind of poetry new to Canadians, but familiar enough to his new milieu, a poetry of passion in which natural emotions are veiled by exotic settings and obscure allusions. This poetry abounds in such language as "our heaven of dream," "the mystical perfection of her kiss," and "the dark rose." It is represented, not unfairly, by such lines as these from "The Rose of My Desire":

> O wild dark flower of woman,
> Deep rose of my desire,
> An eastern wizard made you
> Of earth and stars and fire.
>
> When the orange moon swung low
> Over the camphor-trees,
> By the silver shaft of the fountain
> He wrought his mysteries.

In the sultry atmosphere of his love poems nothing is quite what it seems. To Canadian critics of the time such poetry seemed disquieting and even unwholesome; it is now sufficient to say that it was very much of its time and has nothing whatever in common with the great love poems of that or any other period in literature. Little of it appears in the selection Roberts recently made from his work. It does not form a significant exception to the general truth that Canadian poets have not dealt movingly or naturally with human relationships.

More permanently interesting is Roberts's political poetry. There is, I think, no doubt that his political poetry is the best we have had. In approaching this it is wise to recall that Roberts was for some years a professor of political economy, a chair which he combined with that in English literature at one of the small Maritime colleges; and that he wrote a vigorous popular history of Canada, as well as some romantic historical fiction. For a time at least his attention was given to political facts far more eagerly and constantly than that of any other of our major poets. In his early "Ode for the Canadian Confederacy" he found an accent more fervent than any of his predecessors or contemporaries: he calls upon the new nation to attain consciousness of its latent powers:

This North whose heart of fire
Yet knows not its desire
Clearly, but dreams, and murmurs in the dream.
The hour of dreams is done.   Lo, on the hills the gleam!

Awake, my country, the hour of dreams is done!
Doubt not nor dread the greatness of thy fate.

It appeared that a national poet had arisen.   If he was not specific in his exhortations, at least he pled for:

. . . a patriot people, heart and hand
Loyal to our native earth, our own Canadian land.

If Roberts is without the clear programme that marks some of the political verse of Charles Mair, an active associate in political movements, it must be said that his note of intensity in urging pride in the nation's character and future was a more poetic service to Canada than the most carefully articulated programme could have been.   Stuart Sherman has said of *Leaves of Grass* that the incomparable contribution of Whitman was that he had gone about all over America, picking up one thing after another and insisting how beautiful it was.   Roberts is not a Whitman: no Canadian poet has yet rendered to Canada the service that *Leaves of Grass* rendered to the United States.   Roberts, however, does look at Canada as a whole and does say that what he is looking at is of the very first order: and to say that, meaning, as it does, that Canada is no mere colony, no offshoot or tributary, is to take the first big step towards making a Canadian *Leaves of Grass* possible.   The service that Roberts does us is comparable with the service rendered to the United States by the political verse of Lowell or Emerson.   As Roberts grew older England and the Empire took a larger place in his thought; and though even in 1927 he continued to set Canada first, the note of intense pride and absolute devotion that sounds in the "Ode for the Canadian Confederacy" is not recaptured in any of his late political verse.

It is wrong to say of Roberts, as Cappon does, that in him the man outlived the poet.   Much of his most accomplished verse belongs to his later years; and after he had passed seventy he could write of nature—the surface of nature—with almost as much power as when he was young. Nevertheless, the study of his later poems is disappointing, for a number of reasons.   Inadequacy of thought is more painful in the kind of poetry an older man writes; versatility of mood is less satisfying when the poet has lost the suggestive power of his youth and offers statements instead of evocations; and, finally, it is sad to find a poet of such promise, a poet who was once a founder, a breaker of trails, in the very rear of the modern movement.   The conservatism of Roberts was a factor in his rendering of what was his chief service in the twenty years after he returned to Canada.   He became more and more the spokesman for literature in English Canada.   His prestige as the beginner of the richest movement our literature has ever known, his record in prose of the animal life of the land, his national verse, and the vigour and colour of his character were powerful reasons why he should have been accorded his final role.

One of Roberts's earliest poems, written when he was only eighteen, was his "Epistle to Bliss Carman."   Carman, his cousin, passed through the same high school and the same university, a couple of years behind Roberts. He, too, read widely in ancient literature and in the English poets of the nineteenth century; he, too, began to write as a poet of the senses in love with music and imagery; and he, too, was in love with the nature immediately about him. However, even the earliest poetry of Carman is easily distinguishable from *Orion* and the following collection.

The note of "Low Tide on Grand Pré," which Carman
sought to maintain throughout the entire volume to which
it gave a name, is indeed a unique note, and not only in
Canadian poetry. No one else has ever written quite in
the manner of:

> The sun goes down, and over all
>   These barren reaches by the tide
> Such unelusive glories fall,
>   I almost dream they yet will bide
> Until the coming of the tide. . . .

> Was it a year or lives ago
>   We took the grasses in our hands,
> And caught the summer flying low
>   Over the waving meadow lands,
>   And held it there between our hands?

In its quiet delight in nature, its idyllic imagery and dreamy
music, its perfect relaxation and unbroken gentleness of
tone, this is all of a piece, and the piece is perfect. Perfection is not what Roberts offers.

Of all Carman's merits the beauty of his music is the
most remarkable: his first collection is one of the most
musical volumes of verse in the entire century. Again
and again the ear is excited by such magical phrases as
"Golden Rowan of Menalowan" or "The Trail Among
the Ardise Hills." Sometimes, more often in the work of
his youth, entire poems have a musical perfection. Once
heard, the stanzas I am about to quote are unforgettable:

> Now the lengthening twilights hold
> Tints of lavender and gold,
> And the marshy places ring
> With the pipers of the spring.

> Now the solitary star
> Lays a path on meadow-streams,
> And I know it is not far
> To the open door of dreams.

> Lord of April, in my hour
> May the dogwood be in flower,
> And my angel through the dome
> Of spring twilight lead me home.

The soft, rich music of these lines will dissatisfy only those whose doctrines or sensibilities recoil from this kind of music: of its sort it is perfect.   Carman often falls short of attaining this effect, for which he so generally strives. Of all our major poets, he had the least capacity for self-criticism, the strongest tendency to "run on."   In his other musical vein, a familiar, rather shrill vein, he is seldom altogether happy.   None of his poems is better known than one that illustrates this vein and Carman's failure with it, the "Spring Song" in *Songs from Vagabondia*, with its celebrated beginning:

> Make me over, mother April
> When the sap begins to stir!

Those lines do not exemplify either the music, or the diction, of the piece; more typical is such a stanza as this:

> Only make me over, April,
> When the sap begins to stir!
> Make me man or make me woman,
> Make me oaf or ape or human,
> Cup of flower or cone of fir;
> Make me anything but neuter
> When the sap begins to stir.

The word for that movement and manner is jaunty; and it is scarcely possible to be poetic and jaunty.   The jaunty manner is an impure manner.   It will be more evident perhaps that this is so if we pause on another aspect of Carman's jauntiness, his jauntiness in diction.   "Neuter" is jaunty, and so is "oaf": these are words that can be used in serious verse (as distinguished from light-hearted satire such as Burns could write so masterly) only when the intention is bitter. Pope could have used them, or Browning, but in their hands the terms would have had a searing force. Carman uses them playfully, just as he uses his jaunty poetic manner playfully. The worst about them is not merely that they are unpoetic—which is arguable endlessly—but that they are cloying.

This word brings us to the central weakness of Carman. His poetry as a whole is cloying. The truth of this complaint has occurred even to so worshipping an admirer as Odell Shepard. Mr. Shepard regrets Carman's notion of each of his volumes as a perfect unity:

> Twenty variations upon one tune with very minute and gradual modulations from key to key, leave a final impression less sharply defined than the original theme might have given if left to stand alone. As one reads a volume of verse put together on this principle he is likely to feel that the poet is suffering from some mild obsession or monomania. . . . Because of the lack of contrast in mood and material the reader comes to forget and ignore the poet's subject and to surrender himself to the intoxication of rhythm and the wavering phantasmagoria of poetic images.

In mitigation Mr. Shepard pleads that the tone of one collection differs enormously from that of another, and that in consequence if Carman is read as a whole he will satisfy us of the variety of his poetry and appear as "a poet of very extraordinary range and as one who has done memorable work in each of the many kinds of poetry he has written." This claim cannot, I think, be wholly accepted. What is true is that Carman is reasonably versatile in his choice of subjects, no more so, however, than Roberts, and much less so than Mr. Shepard's praise would suggest; but it is also true that in turning from one of his nature lyrics to one of his elegies and then to one of his dreamy meditations, what strikes one is not the change in subject but the sameness in manner. He is always trying to cast almost exactly the same spell; and before long we become uneasy and the spell ceases to take effect. The monotony that Mr. Shepard admits as a trait in the several collections is a trait of the work as a whole.

It is worth inquiring into the causes of this monotony. In the first place Carman lacks the mastery of pictorial detail that marks all his chief Canadian contemporaries. In his poetry it is seldom that a scene is clearly and sharply drawn, all his autumns are the one hazy autumn, all his sunrises the one golden sunrise. More fatal still is his incapacity for restraint: what would have been charming and, to use Mr. Shepard's word, memorable, loses its effectiveness because, instead of being said firmly and finally, it is played with through stanza upon stanza until the reader has only two feelings, that the music is charming but soporific, and that there is no reason why it should ever cease. The thought is almost always exceedingly tenuous: a vague transcendentalism similar to Roberts's. It is true that out of transcendentalism great poetry can come; but only when transcendentalism is very strongly felt by the poet. If the idea that all is one, and the idea that nature corresponds with spirit, and the idea that man is an element in the world soul strike the poet with a shock of immense surprise, making him feel that his eyes have been suddenly unsealed, then great poetry may emerge. But Carman takes transcendentalism lightly: to him it is all so obvious. And from transcendentalism taken lightly no poetry can come, except an occasional verse or at most a brief lyric. And it is Carman's briefest lyrics that in the main make his best work.

Growing up in Fredericton, in the shadow of Roberts and Carman, ten years their junior, Francis Sherman, like Carman, did his best work in brief lyrics. His poetic career began vigorously: between 1896 and 1900 he issued six books and brochures, the first of them, *Matins*, the most variously promising. Although he lived on until 1926 no more publications followed; and the last piece that the editor of his *Complete Poems*, Dr. Lorne Pierce, could discover dates from 1901. Much of Sherman's energy was taken by his business duties—he rose to be an assistant general manager of the Royal Bank of Canada; but in the claims of business one cannot find an adequate explanation for his long silence. Nor can such an explanation be found in his personal tragedy—his fiancee fell a victim to infantile paralysis and after years of invalidism died—to many poets such tragedies have brought larger utterance and greater fertility. It may be supposed, perhaps, that Sherman appreciating how narrow his vein was, and too fastidious to care for such pale reiterations as have marked the middle and elder years of so many Canadian poets, preferred silence. There is a delicate Pre-Raphaelitism in most of his best poems, not so vivid or suggestive as in Duncan Campbell Scott's early work, but genuine and charming. And in other pieces there is a powerful lyrical impulse which lends to his usually dreamlike spirit a bounding energy. His glass was small, but now and then he drank from his own glass.

The two most powerful and satisfying poets of the period, Lampman and Scott, I am reserving for treatment at greater length in special chapters. If Canadian poetry has any masters, Lampman and Scott are of the company.

III

Though Lampman's fame was growing after his untimely death, though Carman and Roberts were moving along new paths, though Scott was reaching the height of his power, the early years of the new century were dominated by a poetry quite different from theirs, a poetry which set little value on the refinements of pure art, and showed little interest in nature, but fastened upon the simplest intensities of human feeling and action. Greatly as they differed one from another, W. H. Drummond, Robert W. Service and Tom MacInnes all sought to make man the theme of their work and to show man in the raw. They failed to give to our poetry a permanent new direction; but they did acquire for poetry a largely expanded audience. Drummond and Service were more popular than any Canadian poets before or since. That such poetry should conquer where the more delicate art of Lampman and Scott had failed is not surprising if one recalls the note characteristic of Canadian life in the first decade of the present century. It was a period of quick and fevered expansion, a decade of hope, the age when Canadians spoke fluently of having only scratched the surface of the territory that awaited their exploitation.

Drummond was an Irish-born doctor who settled in Quebec Province and came to know the intimate life of French Canadians on the farm and in the village as no English Canadian but a physician could. He became aware how new to other English-speaking persons was the kind of material he was amassing in the course of his professional and social visits; and little by little he began to give it an artistic form. "It seemed to me," he says, "that I could best attain the object in view by having my friends tell their own tales in their own way, as they would relate them to English-speaking auditors not familiar with the French tongue." What this means is best made clear by an example:

> Mos' ev'ry day raf' it is pass on de rapide
>   De voyageurs singin' some ole chanson
> Bout girl down de reever—too bad dey mus' leave her
>   But comin' back soon wit' beaucoup d' argent.

There are more French words here than in most passages of this length; but the general mixture of French words, English words pronounced with a French twist, an occasional French construction, is representative of Drummond's verse as a whole.   In 1897, when he had found by giving informal recitations that there was an audience for what he had written, he gathered together a sample of his work and had it published in New York under the title, *The Habitant and Other French Canadian Poems*.   To make sure of a sympathetic reception from French Canada, he invited a preface from Louis Fréchette, the leading French Canadian poet of the day.   Fréchette seized Drummond's artistic problem with real insight, and commented upon the novelty and difficulty of undertaking to present a group of characters who cannot read even their own idiom and who use a language which is not their own and which they have learned by hearing it spoken.   He was concerned to point out that Drummond had no thought of ridiculing his subjects but was instead bent upon commending them to the respect and affection of English Canada.

It was wise of Drummond to obtain this preface; but it did not suffice. Many French Canadians have never forgiven him for putting a patois on the lips of his habitants, and insist—mistakenly—that the vulgar error in English Canada that French Canadians do not generally speak good French has its origin in Drummond's poems.   The political shortcoming of his work—it was certainly no part of his intention to produce such an effect—is not so grave as its literary weakness.   A stanza such as I have quoted aims at rigorous realism of diction; and this consorts well with the sly humour expressed.   But when Drummond aims at pathos or tragedy—as he does not often do in his first collection—there is an inescapable incongruity between the medium and the substance.

For younger readers, despite his four volumes, Drummond is now scarcely a name, certainly no more; but almost every Canadian knows, usually without recalling who wrote it, the stirring ballad called "The Wreck of the *Julie Plante*." Lines like:

> De cook she's name was Rosie,
>   She come from Montreal,
> Was chambermaid on lumber-barge
>   On de Grande Lachine Canal.

or

> De win' can blow lak' hurricane
>   An' s'pose she blow some more,
> You can't get drown' on Lac St. Pierre
>   So long you stay on shore.

have become parts of the meagre treasure of our popular song. Their author will not always be so neglected as he has been during the last generation.

Service is a marginal figure: his Canadian years were relatively few; and if it were not for the Canadian themes of so many among the most effective of his pieces, there would be no tendency to regard him as a part of Canadian literature. He caught a noisy, highly coloured moment in our history—the Yukon gold-rush—in his noisy, highly coloured verse. Kipling is obviously his master—the Kipling of the early ballads—and he is not much below that Kipling except in the refinements of technique. Like Drummond, he was able, by the vigorous humanity of his subjects and the simplicity of his form, to attract many thousands who would not open books of lyric verse. He has held his audience better than Drummond, but recent Canadian poetry owes nothing to what he did. The narratives of E. J. Pratt or of Watson Kirkconnell do not bear his stamp.

Never so broadly popular as Drummond or Service, Tom MacInnes shares with them a delight in the natural man, whom he conceives not as idyllic, with Drummond, or heroic, with Service, but as bohemian. His best work is not in his narratives, which in language and movement smack of Kipling, Service and Masefield, and show little power in the handling of a tale or the setting of a scene, but rather in his poems of comment. In these he usually employs elaborate forms: very often the ballade, in which his note is almost always serio-comic; or the villanelle, where he is softer and graver; or, now and then, some form of his own devising and naming, such as the *mirelle* or the *cantel*. It amused MacInnes when an academic critic reproved him for his "Mirelle of Found Money," saying that the subject matter was unsuitable to such a form, which, like other of the ancient French forms, called for elegant phrasing and courtly themes. "I made up the name and form of MIRELLE for myself in Montreal, because it sounded that way," he retorted. The mirelle is in five five-lined stanzas, the first stanza rhyming *abaab*, the second *bcbbc*, and so on, till in the final stanza the *a* rhyme recurs in the second and last lines. The cantel is in three four-lined stanzas, the first and last rhyming *aaba*, and the second *bbab*. In general MacInnes uses the mirelle for the same kind of theme and tone as the ballade, and the cantel for the same kind of theme and tone as the villanelle. His gayer manner comes out in such a passage as this stanza from the "Ballade of Detachment":

> Oh damnable palavering
> Of pedagogues too regular!
> I'd rather be a tramp, or sing
> For my living at a bar,
> Or peddle peanuts, far by far,
> Than lose my reasonable ease
> In tow of rule and calendar—
> Among the inequalities.

It is all very *fin de siècle*, London and New York were full of poets who practised this manner, and Carman in his

New York days could do this kind of thing as smoothly, if with less vigorous conviction. The graver manner appears in one of the villanelles, "The Tiger of Desire," more completely perhaps than any other of MacInnes's pieces:

> Starving, savage, I aspire
>   To the red meat of all the World:
> I am the Tiger of Desire!
>
> With teeth bared, and claws uncurled,
>   By leave o' God I creep to slay
> The innocent of all the World.
>
> Out of the yellow, glaring day,
>   When I glut my appetite,
> To my lair I slink away.
>
> But in the black, returning night
>   I leap resistless on my prey,
> Mad with agony and fright.
>
> The quick flesh I tear away,
>   Writhing till the blood is hurled
> On leaf and flower and sodden clay.
>
> My teeth are bare, my claws uncurled—
>   Of the red meat I never tire;
> In the black jungle of the World
>   I am the Tiger of Desire!

That is not MacInnes's most characteristic note; but it is his deepest, and his most original. The melodramatic imagination of the 'nineties is there; but something deeper and truer gives it a special force and the reader a special *frisson*. We are for once out of the world of bars and tramps and easy loves and quaint humours, out of MacInnes's other world of voluptuous dreams and sensuous longings. The elaborate antique form holds within firm restraint a feeling which is at once dangerously fierce and dangerously vague. Completely satisfying poetry is not

written after this fashion, but there is nothing in Drummond
or Service that equals this piece, or one or two others among
MacInnes's shorter poems.

The work of our romantic naturists was to have a final
phase of great refinement in the poetry of Marjorie Pickthall.   Twenty years their junior, she was brought out from
England as a child; and in 1913, when she was thirty, published her first collection.   Canadian critics had long before
seized on her poems and stories as works of distinction; a
long absence from Canada did not break her ties with the
country in which her imagination had sprouted, and she
returned to spend her last years in painful and abortive
effort to realize her full powers.   More than any other
Canadian poet of this century she was the object of a cult:
the kind of comment she evoked is exemplified in Professor
Broadus's claim: "The untimely death of Marjorie Pickthall (April 19, 1922) deprived Canadian literature of its
purest poet.   The two slender volumes, *The Drift of Pinions*
and *The Lamp of Poor Souls*, contain nothing that will place
her among 'the few, the immortal names,' but they do
reveal a singing voice and a delicate perception of beauty
unparalleled in contemporary Canadian poetry."   Unaca-
demic critics boldly placed her among the few, the immortal
names.   It is now clear that the praise she received was
exuberant.   Her perception of beauty has not the clarity
which is so constant a trait of Lampman and its range is
slighter than Roberts's or Duncan Campbell Scott's.   It is
almost purely Celtic, and indeed the essential influence
pervading her work, as Mr. W. E. Collin has shown abundantly, is that of the Irish poetry of the 'nineties.   She
likes to write of:

The cloud-white thorn and the white cloud blowing together

or

a wild swan calling
From the marshes broad and dim

Of her, as of Cameron, it must be conceded that where there is deviation from the main stream of Canadian poetry, it is not because of originality, but because of closer contact with movements in other countries. Still, Canada was, as I have said, the country of her imagination, the setting which now and then does enable her to make her pictures clear and her feelings sharp and strong.

It is not an accident that the work which is most remembered, the poetic play called *The Wood-Carver's Wife*, has a Canadian setting. More moving than this play, which is shot through with misty Celtic symbolism weakening to its dramatic force and pictorial sharpness, are a few pieces in which Miss Pickthall deals more simply and forcefully with Canadian history and legend. There is, for example, "On Lac Sainte Irénée," where despite a softish beginning,

> On Lac Sainte Irénée the morn
> Lay rimmed with pine and roped with mist

the theme of an Indian fleeing from justice is handled with intensity, the picture of nature and the very rhythm co-operating to strengthen the effect, as in such a stanza as this:

> On Lac Sainte Irénée the moose
> Broke from his balsams, breathing hot.
> The bittern and the great wild goose
> Fled south before the sudden shot.
> One fled with them like a hunted soul,
> And followed ever
> By ford and river
> The little canoe of the lake patrol.

The virtue of that last line, which may seem a little pat, and even melodramatic, can be appreciated when the poem is read as a whole: with slight variation it ends each stanza. Or there is the dramatic monologue in which she presents one of the Jesuit martyrs, Gabriel Lalement. She has caught the priest stepping aside from his Indian band during a portage near one of the upper lakes and dreaming nostalgically of the centres of Canadian civilization during the seventeenth century:

> Do the French lilies reign
> Over Mont Royal and Stadacona still?
> Up the St. Lawrence comes the spring again,
> Crowning each southward hill
> And blossoming pool with beauty   .   .   .

and then projecting himself rather wearily into his grim future:

> My hour of rest is done;
> On the smooth ripple lifts the long canoe;
> The hemlocks murmur sadly as the sun
> Slants his dim arrows through.
> Whither I go I know not, nor the way,
>
> Dark with strange passions, vexed with heathen charms,
> Holding I know not what of life or death;
> Only be Thou beside me day by day,
> Thy rod my guide and comfort, underneath
> Thy everlasting arms.

The lines twist and quiver with restrained feeling; the language is apt for the record of the quite simple but quite intense state of mind she is mirroring; and the biblical note, which often sounds a little false in her work, rings true and clear.

After the Celtic influence, the biblical is next in strength. She is bewitched by the biblical parallelisms, and by the biblical imagery melting into music. Biblical themes attract her again and again; and she treats them with a rich orientalism and a never-failing delight in what is very much of the past. All her poetry, except a few brief lyrics, is poetry of the past: the immediate present she was quite helpless to apprehend in its poetic significance.

Even when the war forced itself upon her consciousness and she wrote a once famous sonnet, "Canada to England," she began by hailing

> Great names of thy great captains gone before

and ended by evoking

>   the invulnerable ghosts
> Of all past greatnesses.

When she thought of what the war was fought to preserve she symbolized what she valued by a daffodil. When she thought of what soldiers in German prisons were deprived of, she gathered together images of birds and squirrels, stars and the new moon, trees, the aroma of burning leaves and of the rich earth, and the play of the sun on English beeches. When she was faced with the need to sum up civilization, she summed up nature; for her there was nothing else. And the nature she loved was nature in her exquisite little details.

Naturism could go no farther. Marjorie Pickthall had worked the last and smallest lode. It was time for a change.

IV

The poetry of Drummond, Service and MacInnes was swept aside after the First Great War. It has not counted as an influence since 1918. The war brought a brief stimulus to poetry in Canada as in England; elder poets such as C. G. D. Roberts and Duncan Campbell Scott were stirred to exquisite laments; a few younger writers wrote lyrics with some quiet and lofty beauties; nothing good was achieved in the harsher manners; the one masterpiece was Colonel McCrae's "In Flanders Fields," where careful art, studied moderation in tone, and intense as well as perfectly representative emotion fused to produce a moment's perfection. The poetry of the war was also swept aside; and when the new movements began they were in rivalry with Miss Pickthall and with the nature-verse of Lampman and Scott, Carman and Roberts. It should be remembered that of these five only Lampman was dead—all the others were still writing poetry similar in tone and virtue to their highest achievements.

During the 'twenties foreign travel was easier for young Canadians than it had ever been before. Most of those who have gained reputation in Canadian letters since the end of the first world war have studied or lived in England or France. In their decisive years they underwent pressures which weakened their nationality; and they in most instances elaborated a cosmopolitanism, more or less lasting, in which elements of grace, disillusionment and cynicism combined in a fashion new to Canadian culture. Romanticism was out of favour; and all too often the aversion from romanticism included the romantic past of Canada, the remote past of the explorers, martyrs, and *coureurs du bois* of the French regime, the pioneers, soldiers, and political rebels of the first century of British rule. If the romantic aspects of the Canadian past were not in favour, the sober-suited freemen of the era of Macdonald and Laurier, bourgeois to the core, aroused a more intense repulsion. The solution which appealed to the new generation was the worship of difficult form, and the assimilation of foreign modes of thought and feeling.

Against the elder poets the sad young men rose in angry revolt; they were punctually insulted in the radical journals as the "maple tree school." The bitter vengefulness with which they were harried by the generation of their grandchildren is at first exceedingly difficult to understand. In the perspective of time it is clear that the elder poets had all a high concern with craftsmanship, a preoccupation

with genuineness of feeling, and a belief, not shared when
they began to write by the majority of their English-
speaking compatriots, that the development of a distinctive
Canadian nationality was under way.   In them the younger
poets and critics chiefly disliked two things.   The elder
poets had dealt rather flaccidly with individual character.
Surprisingly little of their work was dramatic or psychological.   When they abandoned nature it was usually to
meditate dreamily on life in general or to exhort.   In none
of them can one find anything in the manner of Frost's
"Death of the Hired Man" or Robinson's "Tasker Nor-
cross."   What the younger men did not sufficiently remember was that even in fiction and in biography Canadians had
failed to deal firmly and vividly with character.   The
second objection was against the form of the elder poets.
To read what was said about it in the 'twenties one would
suppose that the elders had held primly aloof from any
measure more modern than the Spenserian stanza or the
rhyme royal.   The truth is more complex.   All the elder
writers, and notably Scott and Carman, were experimental;
but they had all come under the influence of the rich music
of Swinburne and Verlaine and accordingly retreated from
any roughness of texture.   Moreover, their long-established
prestige did make it painfully hard for younger poets,
penetrated by the alien method and tone of Eliot, Hopkins
and the Metaphysicals, to get a respectful hearing.

The renewal of our poetry after the war had two
independent sources: one man in Toronto and a coherent
group in Montreal.   E. J. Pratt is the pre-eminent figure
in Canadian poetry between the wars: his first important
volume, *A Book of Newfoundland Verse*, belongs to 1923,
the first in which his originality and power were mature,
Titans, belongs to 1926; since the latter date his place has
been uncontested.   His work is reserved for extended
consideration in a special chapter.   In Montreal, in the

early and middle 'twenties, an original group of undergraduates conducted literary magazines far out of the
common run; notable among them was *The McGill Fortnightly*, the most interesting literary magazine English
Canadian students have ever developed. In its pages
appeared most of the early verses of Abraham Klein, Frank
Scott, A. J. M. Smith, and Leo Kennedy who from outside
McGill joined in their quest of strictly contemporary themes
and forms. They were all experimenters, eager to naturalize
in Canada the kind of poetry then being written by Eliot
and Pound, all zealots for the metaphysical verse of the
seventeenth century, then being reinterpreted in Eliot's
criticism, and for Emily Dickinson.   Out of their fellowship
there was to come long afterwards the little anthology,
New Provinces, Poems by Several Authors, in which Pratt
and another Toronto poet, Robert Finch, also appeared.
Three of the Montreal group have brought out collections
of their verse, Leo Kennedy *The Shrouding* in 1933, Abraham Klein *Hath Not a Jew . . .* in 1940, and A. J. M.
Smith *News of the Phoenix* in 1943.   Poetry of the same sort
as theirs is to be found in Dorothy Livesay's *Sign Post*
(1932) and *Day and Night* (1944) and in Anne Marriott's
The Wind Our Enemy (1939).   The poetry of the Montreal
group and of their disciples and associates is the core of
Canadian verse during the past twenty years.   Pratt, it
must always be remembered, is a man apart: his poetry
has invigorated and liberated others, but its influence is
and must be an impalpable one.

Of the Montreal group, Leo Kennedy is much the
simplest.   His range is narrow.   His best poetry has to do
with three themes—the ecstasy of sexual love, the horror of
death, the mystery of resurrection.   When he thinks of love
he usually thinks of death and resurrection; and when he
thinks of death he thinks of resurrection; the three themes
are really phases of one great theme—the cycle of life.

There is a similar narrowness in the range of form in which he is at his best: but whatever his stanza may be, and there is considerable variety in stanza, his movement is rapid, confident, almost ebullient. When he attempts a grave or emphatic movement the vitality and charm evaporates. Vitality and charm he has, at his best, in a remarkable intensity in such lines as

> Now that leaves shudder from the hazel limb,
> And poppies pod, and maples whirl their seed,
> And the squirrels dart from private stores to slim
> The oak of acorns with excessive greed

or

> Hawthorns bloom whitely, laburnums shudder
> Profusion from dim boughs—slight daffodils
> Defy the pale predominance of colour.
> April is rather a month for subtle spells.

The lines abound in massed consonants; still they summon one to pronounce them quickly; and the result is that the lines resound with an extraordinary intensity, and seem tremendously alive. Kennedy himself has a swift, nervous habit of speech and he has found a movement that exactly fits his own temperament. Born a little earlier, he would doubtless have been an almost pure romantic; but his associations with Frank Scott and Arthur Smith led him to explore Sir James Frazer and T. S. Eliot, and, seen through Eliot's eyes, the tragedies and lyrics of the early seventeenth century. He was thus enabled to escape from purely lyric verse into more general statements about love, death and resurrection, and to do so when he was still very young. The perfect expression of the young Kennedy under the influences I have described is in his "Words for a Resurrection":

Each pale Christ stirring underground
Splits the brown casket of its root,
Wherefrom the rousing soil upthrusts
A narrow, pointed shoot,

And bones long quiet under frost
Rejoice as bells precipitate
The loud ecstatic sundering,
The hour inviolate.

This Man of April walks again—
Such marvel does the time allow—
With laughter in His blessèd bones,
And lilies on His brow.

The stamp of Eliot is clear on almost every line, sometimes
in a word, sometimes in an image, sometimes in a movement, but there is a straining eagerness in that last stanza
which is Kennedy's own, and which is essential to the
emotion the poem produces.   That eagerness comes from
the rich romanticism of Kennedy's own self, which no study
could remove.

It is not at all easy to be sure just what Kennedy means
by the resurrection he here celebrates so joyously; but
consideration of his other resurrection pieces leads one to
suppose that what he exults in is simply the endless con-
tinuance of material being, a concept which softens,
although it does not abolish the horror he finds in the
processes that go on in the tomb.   The section of *The
Shrouding* in which "Words for a Resurrection" comes is
significantly entitled "Weapons Against Death."

Much of the work in *The Shrouding* is somewhat careless.   Kennedy is an impetuous poet, and one is sure that,
like Byron, he resembles the tiger who, if his first spring
is not successful, must return to his lair and start all over
again.   In his more recent poems he has turned away from
Eliot and the seventeenth century.   In 1937, moved by the
Spanish War, he called upon the poets to realize:

You are part of the turmoil, Eagles, knit to its glory.
There is work for your strong beaks and the thundering wings,
For the clean flight of the mind and the sharp perception:
There is only a glacial death on the lonely crags.

Obedient to his own advice, he has written simply, ardently
and sympathetically, with just an occasional phrase whose
intricacy and allusiveness suggest his earlier masters.

Whatever kind of poetry Abraham Klein may write,
he always writes as a Jew. Like the other members of the
Montreal group, he underwent the influence of Eliot; but
usually in the moments when he is nearest to Eliot, he is
also richly and vigorously Jewish. His early work was
never better than in the "Soirée of Velvel Kleinburger,"
where the likeness to the Eliot of "Prufrock" and the
"Portrait of a Lady" is obvious. The first few lines are
pure early Eliot:

> In back-room dens of delicatessen stores,
> In curtained parlours of garrulous barber-shops,
> While the rest of the world most comfortably snores
> On mattresses or on more fleshly props

but it is not long before we are restored to a Jewish world,
of

> . . . teachers
> With dirty beards and hungry features

of factories with operatives

> having trickled sweat, according to a scale of wages,
> Sewing buttons to warm the navels of your business sages,

and of social revolutionary dreams. The poem's thread is
a card-game and as the end approaches the significance of
the game is steadily expanded, until Klein makes his mature
and profound comment in an adaptation of a nursery
rhyme:

Hum a hymn of sixpence,
A tableful of cards
Fingers slowly shuffling
Ambiguous rewards.

When the deck is opened
The pauper once more gave
His foes the kings and aces
And took himself the knave.

Juxtaposed with this whimsically expressed wisdom is
Velvel's foolish reverie:

Once more he cuts the cards, and dreams his dream:
A Rolls-Royce hums within his brain;
Before it stands a chauffeur tipping his hat,
'You say that it will rain, Sir; it will rain!'
Upon his fingers diamonds gleam,
His wife wears gowns of ultra-Paris fashion,
And she boasts jewels as large as wondrous eyes,
The eyes of Og, the giant-king of Bashan.

That last touch is the perfect example of how Klein can
use whatever the early Eliot can teach, and yet remain the
Jew, and by remaining the Jew, as Ludwig Lewisohn has
said, contribute something quite new to English poetry.
In substance and form there is so much that is imitative;
and yet the authentic indestructible Jewishness of Klein
has enabled him to convert much of what he borrowed to
his own, already peculiar ends. Here and there in the
early poems there is verbal and rhythmic imitation; but
as he grew older this was to disappear.

If one is not Jewish, Klein's decision to turn away
from the subject and method of the "Soirée" in the direction of Jewish history and legend must be a sharp disappointment. In *New Provinces*, along with the "Soirée,"
he chose to represent himself by a sequence of lyrics on
Spinoza, named "Out of the Pulver and the Polished Lens,"

and in some of these he is indicating the kind of poetry he will in future write.   It is the poetry of a Jew who turns in discontent from the cosmopolitan world around him, exemplified in the first piece in *Hath Not a Jew . . .* by the circle of the Mermaid Tavern, to the world of his own people, exemplified in the great rabbis.   The Christians he presents are cruel oppressors, from Polish barons who think nothing of ordering the slaughter of Jews, to Montreal bourgeois who can never forget that their Jewish friends are Jews.   Over against the Christians who are seen always from the outside he sets a Jew-world which is full of charm and kindness.   A learned man himself, Klein is specially eager to show that the great rabbis were no dried-out killjoys but men in whom life and gaiety\were abundant: the Baal Shem Tov, who found more piety in a child's song under the open sky than in a prayer chanted by ten men in a synagogue, and seeing a child crying bore him to school on his back and quieted his grief by crossing a stream upon his handkerchief; the rabbi Elijah who wished to whoop the moon down from the skies so that he could roll it like a hoop, and the stars so that he could juggle them like marbles; Reb Paupa

> whose belly so did wax
> It sheltered a camel, hump, and load of flax

or he whose complacent ardour in teaching was such

> I think that in Paradise
> Reb Simcha, with his twinkling eyes,
> Interprets, in some song-spared nook,
> To God the meaning of His book.

The picture is charming and familiar: we are at home where we before felt strange; and this is so because Klein has reached down to find something that is universal under the oddities he heaps up.   How true this is will appear by

contrast if one looks at the poems in which Klein presents
the ceremonies of his religion: here there is a surface richness
which may charm for a moment, but there is no power to
universalize the seemingly odd and strange.   Very much
of the collection is given to poetry of this kind.   More
goes to nursery verse, in which affection lends some vitality
to a texture which is without Klein's usual distinction and
force.   As Leon Edel has pointed out, there is much
negligence in the simpler poems and simpler passages in
Hath Not a Jew . . ., so much indeed that in general the
volume may be said to fall short of what "Out of the Pulver
and the Polished Lens" had promised.

As an achievement that poem does not wholly satisfy;
some of its sections are without adequate development of
theme and the thread of the poem's development from
beginning to end is broken more than once.   But in it are
some of the best passages in our poetry between the wars,
passages such as this from the psalm which composes
section VIII:

The wind through the almond-trees spreads the fragrance
of thy robes; the turtle-dove twittering utters diminutives of
thy love; at the rising of the sun I behold thy countenance.

Yea and in the crescent moon, thy little finger's finger-
nail. . . .

Wherefore I said to the wicked, Go to the ant, thou sluggard,
seek thou an audience with God.

On the swift wings of a star, even on the numb legs of a
snail, thou dost move, O lord.

A babe in swaddling clothes laughs at the sunbeams on the
door's lintel; the sucklings play with thee; with thee Kopernik
holds communion through a lens.

or this from section IV, where Klein is close to the Gautier
stanza Eliot has so often used:

> Soul of Spinoza, Baruch Spinoza bids you,
> Forsake the god suspended in mid-air
> Seek you that other Law, and let Jehovah
> Play his game of celestial solitaire.

In his second volume, *The Hitleriad*, the satirist is in command. The title echoes eighteenth century poems; and the masters who have shaped the style and tone are above all Dryden, Pope and Byron, so often in his satires an *attardé* of the Augustan age. It is inevitable that the plight of the Jews should be stressed, but it is stressed much less than Klein's earlier work would lead one to suppose. This is the least Jewish of his longer poems. In the early verses he calls himself

> a grandson of the prophets

and places himself under their aegis, praying:

> Let anger take me in its grasp; let hate,
> Hatred of evil prompt me, and dictate

but despite the spate of invective this is not a prophetic but a satiric poem. Instead of the desperate gravity, the fierce intensity of the prophets Klein offers rather sly contemptuous laughter such as Byron expressed for George III and his ministers. The intellectual defect of the poem is in its making a goose of Hitler. Klein does not allow him any ability at all. How different was Dryden's way! The qualities of the man attacked were fully praised, and the misuse of them, or the dependence on inferior qualities made the object's failure and shame the more appalling. A flock of geese (and Klein treats Hitler's principal associates in the same way as their chief) does not set the world on fire; it takes a great many qualities geese do not have to do that. The sinister cunning of Hitler and Goebbels, the specious force and attractiveness of Goering are forgotten: and the outcome is that the importance of the sub-

ject suffers. But there are many passages of vigorous and
animated verse, and the poem strengthens one's hope that
in later works the full promise of his beginnings will be
realized. That promise was as high as any Canadian poet
has ever given.

Frank Scott, whose father, Frederick George Scott,
was a poet of charm and sincerity, is now professor of
Constitutional Law in McGill University, and one of the
leading humanitarian idealists in Canada; he began with
delicate lyrics of exquisite imagery and muted sound; he
has since filled his verse with a warm and angry concern
for social injustice and social reform. Sometimes, wishing
to appeal to a large and relatively uneducated audience, he
has striven for a simplicity which is almost unpatterned;
again he has contrived to find for his social ideas forms at
once simple and beautifully designed.

Recognized from the outset as the central figure in the
group, A. J. M. Smith proceeded from McGill to Edinburgh
where he undertook graduate studies in the poetry of the
seventeenth century with the counsel of Sir Herbert
Grierson. A professor of English at Michigan State
College, he has shown the strongest critical interest of all
our poets; and in an article contributed to what is perhaps
our main critical journal, *The University of Toronto Quarterly*, he sets forth the tenets of the younger poets with
vigorous simplicity:

> Set higher standards for yourself than the organized medio-
> crity of the authors' associations dares to impose. Be tradi-
> tional catholic and alive. Study the great masters of clarity and
> intensity. . . . Study the poets of to-day whose language is
> living, and whose line is sure. . . . Read the French and German
> poets whose sensibility is most intensely that of the modern
> world. . . . Read, if you can, the Roman satirists. . . .

And remember lastly that poetry does not permit the
rejection of every aspect of the personality except intuition and

sensibility. It must be written by the whole man. It is an intelligent activity, and it ought to compel the respect of the generality of intelligent men. If it is a good, it is a good in itself.

This pronouncement, with which his article concludes, would, I believe, satisfy almost all the younger poets, those in the Montreal group and most of those younger still. The principles he sets forth are embodied in Mr. Smith's own verse.

In the anthology *New Provinces* were twelve of his pieces, varying in their force and beauty from the sharp packed metaphysical imagery in "The Two Sides of a Drum"—

> that country under dream
> Where Eternity and Time
> Are the two sides of a drum

—to the cool conversational manner of Kenneth Fearing in *News of the Phoenix*—

> They say the Phoenix is dying, some say dead.
> Dead without issue is what one message said,
> But that was soon suppressed, officially denied.

News of the Phoenix (1943) is a little book; it holds but thirty-nine poems, spread over about as many pages; and among the thirty-nine are the twelve from *New Provinces*, and others well known to the readers of more recent anthologies of Canadian verse. One had hoped for evidence of greater fertility. A poet who has added but twenty-seven pieces to his canon in seven years, and these the years from thirty-five to forty-two, is either the barren fellow that Johnson called Fielding, or else a most exigent critic.

It is an exigent temperament that this collection reveals, even a haughty temperament. In one of the most admirable poems, Mr. Smith espouses the "cold goddess Pride" and announces that it is to the "barren rock" he addresses his "difficult lonely music." In another, his most explicit exercise in criticism, he counsels a younger writer to aim at achieving the effect

> of a hard thing done
> Perfectly, as though without care.

The tone of that, as well as the idea, recalls the elder Yeats, to whom, in a memorial essay, Mr. Smith paid significant tribute, speaking of him as an "eye made aquiline by thought." Well, Mr. Smith, too, is aquiline, and it is temperament as much as thought, as it was with Yeats, that has made him so.

The eagle's vision is in that picture of the Canadian landscape called "The Lonely Land." This is a scene girt with sharp jagged firs and pines that a ceaseless wind has bent, spume is blown high in the air, and at the centre are wild ducks calling to each other in "ragged and passionate tones." The essence is stirringly caught in these lines:

> a beauty
> of dissonance
> this resonance
> of stony strand.
> this smoky cry
> curled over a black pine
> like a broken
> and wind-battered branch
> when the wind
> bends the tops of the pines
> and curdles the sky
> from the north.

In this harsh world Mr. Smith takes an austere and intense delight. The natural setting for his beautiful "Ode: on the Death of W. B. Yeats" is almost the same. His Ireland has nothing in common with George Moore's or Elizabeth Bowen's: it is no place of soft contours, rich greenery, and

THE DEVELOPMENT OF POETRY 81

gentle rain; his Ireland is the bare hills and rough coast of
Synge, and of Yeats in his elder years. If a tree is conceded blossoms, it is a twisted tree; if a white swan flies
through the poem, the air is cold, and the clouds above
upheave.

Almost equal severity stamps the religious poems with
which the collection closes. In 1936 religion was a minor
theme in Mr. Smith's work, it was scarcely more than an
armoury of imagery. Now it is almost in the dominant
place. The choice of religious topics is revealing: Good
Friday, Calvary, Christian death. A line or two here and
there is infused with gentleness:

> And His face was a faded flower
> Drooping and lost

but lines such as these are among the least successful in
the book. The main effect is that of the Bellini portrait
of Christ: haggard, stricken, at odds with life.

Mr. Smith's theory of poetry leaves an honoured place
for satire and light verse. In the introduction to *The
Book of Canadian Poetry*, he quotes with approval Mr.
Auden's warning that it will "do poetry a great disservice
if we confine it only to the major experiences of life." "Far
West" is a lightly satirical suggestion of a London girl's
feelings as "among the cigarettes and the peppermint
creams" she enjoys a movie about cowboys. More acrid
are "On Reading an Anthology of Popular Poetry" and "Son-
and-Heir." In these Mr. Smith's disgust with bourgeois
values has a searing strength. "Son-and-Heir" is an arraign-
ment of bourgeois civilization in terms of the reveries an
average bourgeois couple might have as they plot the ideal
future for the baby. The quality of the reveries is cheap,
but Mr. Smith would emphasize not only the cheapness,
but the danger of having reveries at all. He is as much
the foe of revery as Irving Babbitt. I mention Babbitt
because the enmity Mr. Smith holds to romanticism is as

deep as Babbitt's: the drubbing he gives to the anthology
of popular poetry shows this to be so. Most of his phrases
of contempt in the poem upon it might be paralleled in
Babbitt, except that Mr. Smith, as a poet, properly
heightens the feeling. He speaks of the "sweet sweet
songs," the "soft melodious screams," the "old eternal
frog in the throat that comes with the words, *Mother,
sweetheart, dog.*" Mr. Smith's satiric poems, more clearly
than any others in the book, make plain the pride and
severity of his temperament. Read first, they will help
prepare one for the emotions that lie within and behind the
more difficult and more important pieces.

Whatever the difficulties it presents, this collection
demonstrates again and again, if not always, not merely
triumphant virtuosity, but perfect keeping between substance and form. It is a book in many manners, but one
can see why there must be many. A proud, hard, noble
and intense book, *News of the Phoenix* makes one regret
that Mr. Smith has not been more fertile, or, if he has kept
much back, that he should not have given us some peeps
into the laboratory in which he works his wonders.

Loosely attachable to the Montreal group are Ralph
Gustafson and Robert Finch. A professor of French
literature, a delicate and deliberate painter, an enthusiast
for modern music, Mr. Finch's preoccupations have been
rather different from those of his Montreal contemporaries.
His verse is full of suggestions of French poets from
Mallarmé down, and his range and use of imagery has
unusual originality and purity. No Canadian poet in our
time has had in greater degree the love of the word or of
design as an autonomous value. His poetry, always
solicitous of musical effect, has steadily moved towards
spareness and simplicity. Mr. Gustafson's art is less
delicate but more brilliant. The impress of Gerard Hopkins' passionate, contorted work and of Anglo-Saxon verse

is upon many of his pieces; fascinating as the Hopkins techniques are in his use of them, one doubts, at times, whether the substance inevitably required so intense and so elaborate a treatment. Whatever question his poetry inspires, Mr. Gustafson is always notable as a curious and striking craftsman.

The best of Dorothy Livesay's poetry is in her latest collection *Day and Night* (1944). Her special power is energy, fiery and at times smoky energy. This energy was early caught up in a passionate devotion to the ideal of a new order:

> O new found land! Sudden release of lungs,
> Our own breath blows the world! Our veins, unbound
> Set free the fighting heart. We speak with tongues—
> This struggle is our miracle new found.

Sometimes the passion for the new order does liberate her, and allows her energy to express itself unimpeded. In the choral passages in the title poem, written as long ago as 1935, the rhythms have a triumphant note even when the substance is resentful and protesting. It is not easy to get free of the beat in:

> One step forward
> Two steps back
> Shove the lever,
> Push it back

or

> Use it not
> For love's slow count:
> Add up hate
> And let it mount.

In her elegy for Garcia Lorca the rhythms are not so ready and simple, but they are as powerful; and the poem as a whole has a maturity and complexity of feeling beyond "Day and Night." Miss Livesay's poetic world is not

limited to ideas or to the problems of social organization—
nature, especially in its energy, makes a strong appeal to
her, and she has found images to express this that stamp
her as a poet of delicate as well as strong sensibilities.
Only here and there in her latest collection, especially in
"West Coast" does the curse of flatness which has blighted
so much proletarian verse fall upon her.   Prediction is not
among the purposes of this essay, but I will venture the
suggestion that hers is a poetry which will become more
widely known in the years beyond the war.

A younger writer, coming too late to feel the full
impact of metaphysical verse or of Eliot's earlier manner,
Anne Marriott immediately acquired a solid reputation
with her first work, *The Wind Our Enemy*, which came out
as a chap-book in 1939.   In this poem of about two
hundred and fifty lines is the first striking presentation in
verse of the great droughts of the decade.   After a spirited
prelude in which the themes are suggested, Miss Marriott
paints the wheatfields in their productive glory; she then
reveals the successive effects on the farmers of year upon
year of drought—a wry courage, then a grudging acceptance
of relief, pathetic efforts at communal amusement, decay
of fibre, and yet persisting through all the phases a residue
of indestructible will; the psychological drama is firmly
set against a vivid background of caked earth, shrivelled
grain and gaunt farm-animals.   It is a great subject, one
of the greatest our poets have approached.   The manner
is not quite equal to it; the scraps of conversation in a
singularly impoverished language will not bear the emotional weight assigned to them when they come to interrupt
the passages of high poetry.   More serious is the imperfect
success in welding the varied elements of the poem into a
totality.   It remains true that none of our recent poets
has had a more interesting beginning; and if her second
work, a radio-play with choruses in verse, *Calling Adven-*

turers, fell short of her first, it fell short in ways that show that Miss Marriott was moving towards a greater command of the large variety of elements she uses.   In a third chapbook, *Salt Marsh*, most of the best qualities in *The Wind Our Enemy* reappear; but Miss Marriott has still to take any important step beyond her first achievement.

The newest of new voices is Mr. Earle Birney's in his *David and Other Poems.* "David" is a narrative of a kind new to our poetry, matter-of-fact in manner and, until the crisis is reached, matter-of-fact in substance also.   It is a tale of two young men climbing mountains along the British Columbian coast, David an experienced mountaineer, Bobbie a novice.   The early sections of the poem— it comes just short of two hundred lines—are rich in pictures and impressions, in passages such as

> Then the darkening firs
> And the sudden whirring of waters that knifed down a fern-
>   hidden
> Cliff and splashed unseen into mist in the shadows

and

> Coming down we picked in our hats the bright
> And sunhot raspberries, eating them under a mighty
> Spruce, while a marten moving like quicksilver scouted us

passages which for all their detail are full of vitality and suggestion, urging the reader to participate fully in the experience of the characters.   These early sections carry also a load of learning, the mountaineer's learning of rocks and fossils, a load perhaps heavier than the prevailing note of simplicity requires.   The two characters are securely realized, the relation between them is warm without ceasing to be simple and clear.   The tragedy comes quietly; Bobbie's foothold gives way and David instinctively turns in a trice to steady him; the added strain is enough to make David slide, and at once he is gone.   It is all over in an instant, the quickness an essential part of the effect Mr. Birney is trying to produce. The central scene is yet to come: it is the dialogue between the two when Bobbie has made his way to where David lies partly paralyzed. Mr. Birney has found simple words, brief phrases, which bear the weight of David's plea to be pushed from the ledge on which he is caught and die in a six-hundred-foot drop, and of Bobbie's plea that he wait till help can be brought. Bobbie yields, staggers back to camp, and

> I said that he fell straight to the ice where they found him,
> And none but the sun and the incurious clouds have lingered
> Around the marks of that day on the ledge of the Finger,
> That day, the last of my youth, on the last of our mountains.

It is impossible to over-praise that close: magic has entered in with the last line, giving an unpredictable extension of meaning, and at one stroke raising the experience of the poem to another level where pain and constraint and self-reproach are no longer matter-of-fact but full of tranquillizing imaginative suggestion. "David" does not stand alone. The little collection—twenty-one poems in all—shows repeatedly that in Mr. Birney's work there is authentic originality; he owes nothing at all to earlier Canadian writing and scarcely anything—when he is fully himself—to recent verse anywhere else. He has a harsh and intense sensibility which makes his pictures and rhythms fresh and living, and his technical accomplishment is brilliant, at times bewildering.

More conservative strains have been abundantly represented in the poetry of the past twenty years: a glance through the best anthology of recent Canadian verse, Mrs. Ethel Hume Bennett's *New Harvesting* (1938), will show that the majority of competent verse-writers in Canada have been little affected by the movement which began with the *McGill Fortnightly*. Some of the conservative

writers have struck notes of power, if not of originality:
Mrs. Louise Morey Bowman has written imagist poetry of
real distinction; in "Laodamia" and some shorter pieces
Miss Audrey Alexandra Brown has brought a new richness in colour and sound to romantic narrative and song;
Dr. George Herbert Clarke, notably in his odes, has demonstrated repeatedly a mastery of technique and a feeling for
the grand style; Mr. A. S. Bourinot and Mr. Kenneth Leslie
have written sonnets of musical sweetness and, often, of
intense and finely controlled feeling; Mr. Watson Kirkconnell in his translations (notably from Polish and Hun-
garian) and in his narratives has a happy energy and ease;
Mr. L. A. MacKay—as well as being our most angry and
clever satirist—has written rich, descriptive pieces recalling
Heredia and the middle manner of William Morris; many
members of the Roberts family have written nature verse
accurate, musical and striking, if never approaching the
excellence of their chieftain; perhaps the richest natural
endowment of any of the poets in this group is that of the
most prolific among them by far, Mr. Wilson Macdonald.
He resembles Carman in many ways, in his delight in vague
and subtle music, in his quest of vagabondia, in his preoccupation with his states of mind; in none of these is his
resemblance to Carman closer than in his lack of self-
criticism.   Between the range of his average performance
and that of his few fine lyrics the gap is astonishing; but
when he is at his best he is admirable indeed, intense in
feeling, sensitive in imagery, uncannily musical.

CHAPTER THREE

The Masters

1. ARCHIBALD LAMPMAN

I

IN THE United States and in England the most widely
known and admired of our poets has been Bliss Carman.
In Canada Lampman is the nearest approach to a national
classic in verse, and the passing of decades has confirmed
his status if it has not very much widened the circle of his
readers. Lampman contributed steadily to the literary
magazines in the United States; his reputation at home
was given its impetus by William Dean Howells's review
of his first volume in *Harper's;* and his second collection
was brought out by a Boston publisher; it remains true,
however, that American interest in him was slight and
temporary, and has for long been quite dead. His case
has a special significance for the student of Canadian
poetry, who must inquire whether the praise he has had at
home is supported by the intrinsic merit of his work, and
whether there are special reasons why this poet should be
neglected abroad—for the English, too, make no mention
of him now—reasons which need not perhaps prevent us
from claiming that his poetry deserves to be read everywhere that people care for what is authentic in literature.

Lampman's early verse is a delicate record of the
surface of nature. For the Canadian poet he thought that
nature was the surest of subjects. "In the climate of this

country," he wrote in 1891, "we have the pitiless severity of the climate of Sweden, with the sunshine and the sky of the north of Italy, a combination not found in the same degree anywhere else in the world. The northern winters of Europe are seasons of terror and gloom; our winters are seasons of glittering splendour and incomparable richness of colour. At the same time we have the utmost diversity of scenery, a country exhibiting every variety of beauty and grandeur." And "for the poet the beauty of external nature and the aspects of the most primitive life are always a sufficient inspiration." Sometimes his manner of recording it reflects his close study of Wordsworth, as in the early "Winter Hues Recalled," which abounds in such notations as this:

> Ere yet I turned
> With long stride homeward, being heated
> With the loose swinging motion, weary too,
> Nor uninclined to rest, a buried fence,
> Whose topmost log just shouldered from the snow,
> Made me a seat. . . .

Everything in the manner of this is imitative of "The Prelude," slavishly imitative, if you will; what is significant is that taking so much from Wordsworth as he does, the young poet applies it so surely and so sharply to scenes and situations in his own immediate world, in this instance a wintry field surrounded by a snake-fence and a snow-shoer making his way across, something as Canadian as pea-soup and maple-sugar. It was the same with his borrowings from Keats, the strongest and most lasting influence upon his style and upon his handling of nature. In the first of the poems in the manuscript book from which he made up his first collection occurs the line:

> Mute maker of a soft pale-petalled rhyme

and that Keatsian accent marks more than half of Lampman's early manuscripts. Again, however, he brings his
study of Keats to bear upon his immediate world. He did
not believe that the piece from which this line comes was
worthy of being published; and he also laid aside the poem
from which I shall now take an excerpt, a poem in which
he is trying to catch the quality of a late August day
through which autumn is beginning to make itself felt:

> All day cool shadows o'er drowsy kine
> The wide elms in the windless pasture flung;
> The tufted branches of the sun-soaked pine
>   Grey-silvery in the burning noon-tide hung;
> The light winds clattered in the poplar leaves
>   The squirrels robbed among the golden sheaves.

That sun-soaked pine, those clattering poplar leaves, are
presented with Keats's sensibility; they and the squirrels
and the elms are taken straight from the Ontario landscape.
The desire for sharp accuracy and the nervous sensibility—
these were the great qualities the young Lampman had
within himself; he sought from the English romantics, and
later from Arnold and Tennyson, instruction not in what
to see or how to feel, but in how to express what he saw
and how he felt. It would be fatuous to expect that a
novice could find within himself the secret of adequate
expression: he went to Keats and Wordsworth as Tennyson
did, and as Keats went to Spenser and Shakespeare, and
Wordsworth to Milton. What is remarkable is that like
them he found within himself the secret of vision and
emotion. What one will wish to know is whether as he
became more practised in expression he could emerge from
the tutelage of Wordsworth and Keats and speak to us
directly, sensitively, powerfully, in a personal idiom
mirroring an interesting and original personality.

II

Before we approach the poems in which Lampman's record of nature is at its best, the external factors in his development should be made clear. He came from an extremely conservative environment; indeed it could have been more conservative, more typical of the ascendant party in Upper Canada only by being opulent. On both sides of his family he was descended from Loyalists, and on his mother's side, at least, his ancestors had been men of substance in the American colonies. Lampman's father, a Church of England rector who delighted in the literature of Queen Anne's time, spent his life in small, conservative, southern Ontario towns and villages. The boy was sent to a private school kept by a man who at one time had been headmaster of the principal Tory academy in the province; from this Lampman passed to Trinity College School, which prepared boys for entrance into Trinity University, the Church of England college in Toronto; and in due time Lampman went up to Toronto, not to the provincial university but to Trinity, where he was in company which was prevailingly Tory and Anglican, and under the influence of teachers who were clerics of English birth and education. Every element in his early environment told against the development of Canadianism in Lampman, but Canadianism did develop very early.

One of the most charming pages in our literary history is that in which Lampman tells of his overpowering emotion when, a youth of twenty, he came on the newly published work of another Canadian youth of twenty, the *Orion* of Charles G. D. Roberts:

"Like most of the young fellows about me, I had been under the depressing conviction that we were situated hopelessly on the outskirts of civilization, where no art and no literature could be, and that it was useless to expect that anything great could be

done by any of our companions, still more useless to expect that
we could do it ourselves. I sat up most of the night reading and
re-reading *Orion* in a state of the wildest excitement and when
I went to bed I could not sleep. It seemed to me a wonderful
thing that such work could be done by a Canadian, by a young
man, one of ourselves. It was like a voice from some new paradise of art, calling to us to be up and doing. A little after sunrise
I got up and went out into the college grounds. The air, I
remember, was full of the odour and cool sunshine of the spring
morning. The dew was thick upon the grass, all the birds of our
Maytime seemed to be singing in the oaks, and there were even
a few adder tongues and trilliums still blooming on the slope of
the little ravine. But everything was transfigured for me
beyond description, bathed in an old world radiance of beauty,
the magic of the lines was sounding in my ears, those divine
verses as they seemed to me, with their Tennyson-like richness
and strange earth-loving Greekish flavour. I have never forgotten
that morning, and its influence has always remained with me."

Could a nation's poetic history begin with a more charming
freshness? It is delightful to look back across the years
to that bright spring morning in the semi-wild meadows
about the old Trinity building, to evoke the delicate, young
Ontario poet destined to die long before he had grown to
his full power, reading from the slim booklet of the young
man from New Brunswick who was so recently, after the
passing of more than sixty years, shaping verses in the city
where so long ago Lampman caught from him the assurance
that a Canadian literature was waiting to be born. The
delight he felt in that first volume of Roberts was a delight
springing from his need to feel that Canadians were not,
to use the phrase of Henry James, among the disinherited
of art, to feel that great things of a special sort might be
done here and now. It must, I think, be assumed that
Lampman's Canadianism was of the rarest and most
precious kind, that it was instinctive.

It was destined to grow in circumstances not much

more hospitable than those of his home and education. A few months after leaving college, Lampman entered the service of the federal Post Office at Ottawa, and he was to remain a humble, ill-paid clerk in this department for the rest of his life. In 1883, when he came to Ottawa, Sir John A. Macdonald was Prime Minister; a boom was on; the Canadian Pacific Railway was the nexus of political activity; the sixteen-year-old Confederation was a business civilization. It was impossible for Lampman to interest himself in the typical expressions of Canadian life. A civil servant in a sub-Arctic lumber village converted into a political cock-pit—this was Goldwin Smith's account of Lampman's Ottawa—he saw the seamy side of politics at close range. How complete his disgust was many a line makes plain. As he saw member upon member and minister upon minister play his part in the pit, he concluded that they were indifferent and even defiant towards truth and principle and that for them the administration of a country was a shabby but lucrative game. I am told that he was accustomed to describe the man who was his own minister in the last years of his life as Moloch. Nowhere in his published verse is his contempt for the politician so fierce as in this epigram which he kept to himself and his friends:

> From the seer with his snow-white crown
>   Through every sort and condition
> Of bipeds, all the way down
>   To the pimp and the politician.

Nor did he judge the money-makers more mildly. Again a piece unpublished in his lifetime supplies the strongest evidence, the harsh "Epitaph on a Rich Man":

> He made himself a great name in his day,
> A glittering fellow on the world's hard way;
> He tilled and seeded and reaped plentifully
> From the black soil of human misery.

> He won great riches, and they buried him
> With splendour that the people's want makes grim;
> But some day he shall not be called to mind
> Save as the curse and pestilence of his kind.

Political trickery and financial exploitation seemed to him to be the permanent staples of the city: it bears the curse of gold, the curse of harassed, mindless toil, the curse of shallow, aimless speed. Through the darkness of midnight Lampman hears the mill-wheels turning on the river, and the trains roaring in and out of the station. Nor does he expect that the future will be nobler: in his apocalyptic piece, "The City of the End of Things," originally entitled "The City of Machinery," he projects a Butlerian nightmare of man as victim of mechanical civilization. "The issue of the things that are," as he calls it in a sub-title, is a pandemonium of noise, where

> The beat, the thunder and the hiss
> Cease not, and change not, night nor day.

Man will not be able to sustain life in its mephitic atmosphere: he will be superseded by machines; a carved idol of an idiot will preside over its clangor; and the final state of the city shall be one in which all is destroyed except the huge, idiotic face.

It should now be clear why Lampman retreated from the city. Urban life was in principle defective. As he moved about in Ottawa year after year, as one political administration gave way to another, and one piece of skulduggery surpassed another, only one quality of the city continued to please him: the beauty of buildings. He liked to take his stand on the river-bank or on the hills on the Quebec side, especially at sunrise or sunset, and look back at the great group of buildings which stood even then on Parliament Hill; man-made though they were, he found them congruent with the grandeur and vigour of the landscape into which they melted, adding a new charm. It was the same with St. Catharines, that small city on the Niagara Peninsula which he praises in a sonnet significantly entitled "A Niagara Landscape." Viewing the rich plains and orchards, dotted with towers and dim villages, he finds the scene crowned:

> Far to westward, where yon pointed towers
> Rise faint and ruddy from the vaporous blue,
> Saint Catharines, city of the host of flowers.

Nature drew Lampman not only because it was great and beautiful in itself; but just as much because it was a refuge from the society he had found to be neither. Again and again he sounds the note of nature the refuge; for instance, in his Swinburnian piece, "Freedom," entitled in the manuscript "Out of Prison," he is seeking escape

> Out of the heart of the city begotten
>   Of the labour of men and their manifold hands,
> Whose souls, that were sprung from the earth in her morning,
> No longer regard or remember her warning,
>   Whose hearts in the furnace of care have forgotten
>   For ever the scent and hue of her lands.

If Lampman was a good Canadian, he was so in his own fashion. Whatever might be said of Canadian politics and Canadian society and Canadian character, the Canadian landscape was grand and beautiful—no one could wish for anything grander or more beautiful. For the time at least, he believed, the Canadian poet should make himself its sensitive recorder and thus reflect the nation without tarnishing his poetry. The Canadian poet, he has said, must depend on nature and on himself, and on these alone.

III

It is now easier to consider the question raised some time past—whether Lampman in his approach to nature could free himself from imitation and find an utterance which would carry adequately what he saw and how he felt. Even in his first collection, published when he was twenty-seven, there are passages and a few whole poems in which Lampman is master of his emotion and vision, and speaks for himself. When I first read him the poem which convinced me that he was a poet of authentic distinction was "Heat," written as early as 1883, a piece to which I shall return. The quality of "Heat" is to be found in some of the early sonnets, for instance, "Late November":

The far-off leafless forests slowly yield*
    To the thick-driving snow. A little while
    And night shall darken down. In shouting file
The woodmen's carts go by me homeward-wheeled
Past the thin fading stubbles, half-concealed,
    Now golden-gray, sowed softly through with snow,
    Where the last ploughman follows still his row,
Turning black furrows through the whitening field.
Far off the village lamps begin to gleam,
    Fast drives the snow, and no man comes this way;
        The hills grow wintry white, and bleak winds moan
        About the naked uplands. I alone,
    Am neither sad, nor shelterless, nor gray,
Wrapped round with thought, content to watch and dream.

Lampman's method as landscapist has been carefully studied by Mr. W. E. Collin, who comments on the precision of the details, on "an intangible quietness and repose and warmth" that "linger over the lines and colours," on the selection of words for "their aura of high visibility." To

*Superior I think to the reading in the printed text:
    The hills and leafless forests slowly yield.

keep to terms used in the sonnet that has been quoted, Lampman *watches*, with an eye sharper than any other Canadian poet's, an eye which appreciates not only the contours and colours of particular objects but just as sharply the relations between objects, and Lampman *dreams*, he does not merely record but also feels the essence of the scene in which he finds himself, the essence here of helpless bleakness with a strange, moving beauty of its own. It appears to me that the sensibility this sonnet reveals is a highly personal one, that what Lampman is telling us is something that no one else has quite told us; and it appears to me, also, that he has told us what he had to tell in his own way, that he has escaped from his early masters. "Late November" is great nature poetry.

How much of Lampman's nature poetry is comparable with this sonnet? Keeping still to the first collection, I should say that few of the longer pieces have anything so excellent and that none but "Heat" maintains it throughout. Perhaps the most remarkable work in the volume is a sequence of five sonnets entitled "The Frogs," which expresses the permanent core of Lampman's nature philosophy. These are not the ordinary bull-frogs but those shy creatures whose thin, sweet voices rise in chorus in the early summer from many a pool and swamp in Ontario and Quebec. "Quaint uncouth dreamers, voices high and strange" Lampman calls them; and as he listens to them, in that dreamy mood already noted, he comes to believe that they are the organ by which nature seeks to communicate to us her inmost meaning. Morning, noon, and night they sing to us, as nature tells her simple, deep significance over and over, so that we may be sure to catch it; as we listen we are made to dream, taken out of our ordinary personalities, washed clean of all our preoccupations. Nothing else conserves its reality,

Morning and noon and midnight exquisitely,
Rapt with your voices, this alone we knew,
Cities might change and fall, and men might die,
Secure were we, content to dream with you
That change and pain are shadows faint and fleet,
And dreams are real, and life is only sweet.

There, for the young Lampman, is the whole meaning of
nature; there for him is the truth of life. His sequence
abounds in phrases of the richest suggestiveness, touched
with Keats and Matthew Arnold, but his own, phrases
such as

The wonder of the ever-healing night

Still with soft throats unaltered in your dream.

All of them in the tone that the theme requires, these are of
his own coinage.

IV

One other escape from the routine and meanness that
he detected in his environment was available to Lampman.
For a long time critics have complained of Lampman's
failure to treat of love. MacMechan spoke mildly of the
lack, and a later critic more emphatically insists that "the
love-passion, so conspicuously absent in his poetry, may
have been dried up under the austere respectability of
Ontario and the polite humanism of Matthew Arnold."
And yet one might suppose that to a young man with
Keatsian sensibility, indifferent to the social and economic
currents about him, love and the poetry of love might well
be a preoccupation. To Lampman they were, as his
various manuscripts disclose. Two unpublished narratives, "Arnulph" and "White Margaret," are packed with
love. "Arnulph," the richer of the two, the story of a
vassal's love for his maiden lady, recalls again and again
"The Eve of St. Agnes," in lines such as these:

> I must die, or with my whole soul drink;
> Unless between my hungering arms I fold
> Her whole dear loveliness to have and hold
> Forever, I can no more rest or bear
> This broken life or breathe the sunless air.

Stronger evidence and greater power appear here and there in a sequence of eight sonnets, written in 1884-1885, and reflecting his love for Maud Playter, whom he was to marry. A pair of curtal sonnets of the same period and quality, demonstrably addressed to the same person, are entitled in the manuscript "Praise and Prayer." Where so much is notable for intensity and so little for accomplished art, it is hard to know what should be quoted: probably none of the sonnets is all in all so remarkable as the second in the "Praise and Prayer" set:

> Ah, God were very good to me, I said,
> If this, this only, he would grant for alms,
> That one day I might hold her yellow head,
> With all its locks between my worshipping palms,
> And bend and kiss the innocent lips upheld;
> And the fair cheeks caress from youth to eld.
> Ah me; I would have toiled, as no man did
> Ever on earth, or with a strength divine
> Have braved the whole hard world, if she did bid;
> Only to touch her glorious lips and twine
> Thrice blessèd her two yielded hands in mine,
> And tell her all that in my heart lay hid.

For such poetry or for the elaborate "Arnulph" and "White Margaret" I should not think of claiming the praise that is due to the early nature verse. Lampman's visual powers always desert him when he turns from nature to woman; his sensibility remains acute but his gift of language is sometimes withdrawn from him as it was from Keats. But there is no question, either in this poem or in his love poetry as a whole, that his passion was intense: and his own awareness of the intensity is shown by his having pinned the pages on which these sonnets were written in his manuscript book and requested his friends not to remove the pins when they were going through the collection. That is even more revealing than his decision that only one of the sonnets should be published. The chief interest of this group of poems is psychological: it is important for us to know that love was an early theme of Lampman's, a theme to which from 1884 on he returned again and again. It was to be a long time before another Canadian poet wrote of passionate love with such force.

V

Among the Millet had appeared in 1888; seven years later Lampman brought out a second and slighter collection, *Lyrics of Earth*. It is disappointing that so few of the notes he now strikes are different from those in the earlier book. It is disappointing but I do not think that it is surprising. I have mentioned Lampman's claim that a Canadian poet was dependent solely on nature and on himself. After making that observation, he went on to say:

He is almost without the exhilaration of lively and frequent literary intercourse—that force and variety of stimulus which counts for so much in the fructification of ideas. The human mind is like a plant, it blossoms in order to be fertilised, and to bear seed must come into actual contact with the mental dispersion of others. Of this natural assistance the Canadian writer gets the least possible.

There is no doubt that Lampman is here describing his own case. Duncan Campbell Scott, looking back on his friend's career a quarter century after his death, has told us that Lampman was unusually dependent on the society about him and that if in Ottawa he had found a more stimulating society his achievement would have been greater by far.

It is indicative that Lampman clung so long to the associations that he formed in college, as if failing to discover an
adequate milieu in the capital.   Mr. Scott's picture of
Lampman's life in Ottawa is depressing:

> He felt the oppression of the dullness of the life about us
> more keenly than I did; for he had fewer channels of escape
> [Lampman was not a deep or wide reader, nor was he a musician]
> and his responsibilities were heavier; he had little if any enjoy-
> ment in the task-round of every day, and however much we miss
> the sense of tedium in his best work, most assuredly it was with
> him present in the days of his week and the weeks of his year.
> He had real capacity for gaiety and for the width and atmos-
> phere of a varied and complex life, not as an actor in it perhaps,
> but as a keen observer and as a drifter upon its surface, one in
> whom the colour and movement of life would have created many
> beautiful and enchanting forms.   But he was compelled to work
> without that stimulus, in a dull environment. . . .

In a lecture he gave to the Ottawa Literary and Scientific Society in 1891 Lampman calmly took stock of the
society round about him.   People were too busy to read,
or at least to read in the only way that counts, with discern-
ment.   Schools and even the best universities sent forth
not men of rounded culture, discerning readers, but merely
"smart lawyers, competent physicians, able business men."
These would found fortunes and families, and in a later
time Canada would have a literary market and a literary
atmosphere.   Meanwhile a poet—and it was better to
be a poet than a critic, or a novelist, or a dramatist, for
these would suffer even more acutely from the intellectual
and spiritual shortcomings of their contemporaries—had
himself and nature.   And these were all Lampman had
except for a few friends, notably Mr. Scott and Wilfred
Campbell, with whom, for a year or so, he made a trio to
conduct a literary department in a Toronto daily, and a
small group who were interested in socialist ideals.   Nature

he appears to have felt by 1888 as strongly as he would ever feel her; the very title of the second collection establishes that it, too, is primarily nature verse; and the nature pieces that predominate in it are largely interchangeable with those in *Among the Millet*.   By 1895 Lampman had a firmer mastery of what he had learned from Keats: one has but to compare the "June" of the second volume with the "April" or "Among the Timothy" of the first to appreciate the advance.   In the later pieces the language is more uniformly admirable, and the rhythms a little freer.   But all in all the treatment of nature is almost the same, the idea of nature is exactly the same.   What of the poet's self? Lampman's favoured vehicle for disclosing what was going on within himself was the sonnet; in the first collection there are thirty sonnets, in the second, none.   *Lyrics of Earth* [1895] is a very unreflective book.   The best clue to the poet's mind that it furnishes comes in the long poem, "Winter-Store," written at the close of 1889, where he sets side by side, as he had so often done, the world of nature and the world of man.   In winter pent in the city, he would have his spirit subsist on the sense impressions garnered in the other seasons of the year; as it strives to do so, suddenly the still, sad music of humanity breaks in:

> Yet across the windy night
> Comes upon its wings a cry;
> Fashioned forms and modes take flight,
> And a vision sad and high
> Of the labouring world down there
> Where the lights burn red and warm
> Pricks my soul with sudden stare.

And no fragrant memory of April or June quite suffices to divert his attention from social evil and perversion.   There is no doubt that the longer he lived in Ottawa, and the more he winced at his bondage of clerical taskwork, the surer he became that our constitution of society was incompatible with the good life for man in general.

What the good life was and what it supposed, we shall presently see in some of his later poems. When *Lyrics of Earth* appeared Lampman had only four years to live; and no further collection of his appeared during his lifetime. He did, however, plan a volume to be named *Alcyone and Other Poems* and had even read the final proofs. The pieces it was to consist of have been grouped in the collected edition which by the zeal of Duncan Campbell Scott came out the year after the poet died. As evidence of how Lampman desired to approach his readers in his third trial they deserve corporate consideration, and we shall see that the *Alcyone* volume has much to say about the good life and its opposite.

At first glance it seems very similar to *Among the Millet*, another mixture of sonnets that are chiefly pictorial and atmospheric, rich nature verse, a few lyrical cries and a miscellany of meditative verse. Closer study will disclose that there are notable differences, technical and intellectual. Except in a handful of sonnets, the *Alcyone* collection has not much pure or nearly pure nature poetry: to describe the surface of nature, to catch the tone of a natural scene, to record his own responses to the procession of the seasons and the comings and goings of the birds, is no longer enough. Scott's observation that "the only existence he coveted was that of a bushman, to be constantly hidden in the heart of the woods" has been taken too literally by some critics. All through his life he had moods, often long drawn out, in which he felt exactly as a poet critic has suggested:

> Lampman pronounced the vernal musk
> An adequate relief from thought
> He found the Blue Hills gave a vent
> For all the Civil Service taught.

It is true that at the end as at the beginning, Lampman was happiest when he was melting into the landscape; but at the end he was no longer dependably at peace when he was so lost in nature: the embrace was now a drug and often he both feared and foresaw the awakening. The note predominant in *Among the Millet* was that of tranquil happiness; in *Alcyone and Other Poems*, it is that of intellectual and spiritual struggle.

VI

In tracing Lampman through his last years the sonnets whose first appearance, at least in book form, was in the collected edition are a valuable supplement to the *Alcyone* pieces. They are astonishingly varied in theme, ranging from delicate nature vignettes, through harsh and powerful insights into nature's grander aspects, to reflections, sometimes very forceful, on moral ideas and human oddities. Lampman can still strike the note of Keatsian richness, as in the vivid close of "Across the Pea-Fields":

> Across these blackening rails into the light
> I lean and listen, lolling drowsily;
> On the fence-corner, yonder to the right,
> A red squirrel whisks and chatters; nearer by
> A little old brown woman on her knees
> Searches the deep hot grass for strawberries

Little of such rich work as that last line belongs to the last years. Lampman was then more likely to pierce through the surface to some significance in nature which bore upon man's fate, as in the end of "A Summer Evening":

> Peaceful the world, and peaceful grows my heart.
> The gossip cricket from the friendly grass
> Talks of old joys and takes the dreamer's part.
> Then night, the healer, with unnoticed breath,
> And sleep, dark sleep, so near, so like to death.

This utterance, seven years later than "Across the Pea-Fields," may tell of peace and claim peace, but how uneasy it is, how deeply stirred with gloom in comparison with the earlier poem! Uneasiness runs through many of the moral sonnets such as "Xenophanes" (1892) or "Chaucer" (1894) or "Passion" (1896) or "To the Ottawa River" (1898). Still the uneasiness in the sonnets is restrained by the purity of the form and for the sharpest and fullest expressions of Lampman's anxieties we must turn to the major poems in the *Alcyone* volume. "The City of the End of Things" has already been mentioned; it is perhaps the strongest expression of Lampman's social pessimism. It is not, however, intellectually so impressive as "The Land of Pallas," a long utopian piece where Lampman sets forth his social ideal only to concede that it is unattainable.

The land he dreams of is one where voices are sweet, with the essential sweetness of fine feelings; where houses and gardens are quiet and beautiful; where work goes on in the open air and is followed by kindly festival; where everyone has enough and no one has great wealth or great power; where there is no army, no judiciary, no caste, no marriage, no king; where honour is reserved to the masters of language and wisdom; where one man understands his neighbour as an affinity and is understood in return. As in Erewhon machinery has been scrapped and stored in museums to remind the malcontent of an era of horror. This is the land of Pallas—it is almost Morris's "Nowhere": we could attain it, Lampman says, if we wished; but its advocate is repressed by the rulers of our society as an anarch and by the masses avoided as a madman. Originally this poem, written in 1892, ended on the note of pure despair:

> Then I returned upon my footsteps madly guessing,
>   And many a day thereafter with feet sad and sore
> I sought to win me back into that land of blessing,
>   But I had lost my way, nor could I find it more.

Subsequently Lampman dropped this stanza and struck a note of resolute if limited cheer:

> And still I preached, and wrought, and still I bore my message,
>   For well I knew that on and upward without cease
> The spirit works for ever, and by Faith and Presage
>   That somehow yet the end of human life is peace

Lampman's despair went deep but never so deep as to destroy or even disturb his intuition that the core of the universe is sound. Society can corrupt man and does: Ottawa had almost corrupted Lampman. Man can resist corruption by maintaining close and passionate contact with nature: this Lampman did summer and winter, in fact and in imagination. If, as he says in "The Poet's Song," the fountain should run dry, one has but to hasten to the wilds and the life of the spirit will be renewed. Renewal and resistance to corruption may also flow from that rare accomplishment, reciprocal understanding between two human spirits,

> When ardour cleaves to ardour, truth to truth.

An unpublished dramatic poem written in the poet's later years gives vigorous expression to his belief in the healing value of such understanding. The separated lovers, brought together at the close, by an act of heroic abnegation on the part of the woman's husband, are hailed by the chorus in a final song:

> But here with happy feet returning
>   Come the lovers, Prince and bride,
> Through a magic mist discerning
>   Many gates of life set wide.
>
> In their hearts the mounting paean
>   Of the marriage chorus calls,
> They have seen the Cytherean
>   They have trod her golden halls.

Happy Prince and happy Queen,
  All their doubt and trouble past
In the light of love's demesne
  They have found their tongues at last,
And they talk with linked hands,
Heart to heart that understands.

Social arrangements make it difficult for man to live in the midst of nature; and they may make it difficult for a relation between affinities to realize itself. But reproach should be directed not against nature, not against love, still less against the universe, but simply against society. Lampman's pessimism is purely social.

VII

It should now be evident that in his later years Lampman's conception of life was much more comprehensive than his readers and interpreters have generally supposed. "It is idle to conjecture what the course of his development might have been," Scott declared, unveiling the memorial cairn at Morpeth, "but one can hazard that it would broadly have tended towards the drama of life and away from the picture of nature." It may perhaps be objected that his widening range of interest was not deeply significant for his poetry, that his best work at the end as at the beginning of his life was in his record of the surface of nature and of his responses to it. Undoubtedly the poetic beauty of "The Land of Pallas"—excluded by Duncan Campbell Scott from the selected edition of 1925— is far inferior to the poetic beauty of, let us say, "Heat" or "The Frogs." Is there any poem composed in his last years that can be set beside these nature pieces without suffering by the comparison, a poem reflecting the widening of his interest? I think that nowhere has he gone beyond the poetic beauty of a poem celebrating Daulac and his companions at the Long Sault, a poem on which he was working a few months before his death.

This poem appeared in 1943 as the title piece of a collection of hitherto unpublished poems by Lampman brought out by Dr. Scott and myself. I can never forget the joy I experienced as I deciphered it in the rough note book in which the poet worked it out, scoring out many a word and phrase, and sometimes a whole passage, and several times giving up in despair and starting anew. It is all too easy for the discoverer of a poem such as this to exaggerate its merit; and I have been accused of doing so. One qualified critic finds its epithets often commonplace; another critic whose acerbity makes him less dependable denies that its closing lyric has any great elegiac power. I can only say that I have not been moved from my first opinion that "At the Long Sault" is a masterpiece despite adverse criticism; to look at the poem afresh, to note once more its qualities in substance and form, has been to recapture the elation which pursued me for weeks after I had discovered it in those yellowed and crumbling pages.

He had a great theme—against the background of the Ottawa and the forests, in the spring of 1660, Daulac and his little band of French Canadians held a dilapidated fort for about ten days against an overwhelming number of Iroquois, continuing to fight till all had been grievously wounded and all but four were dead. Their resistance ended an Iroquois project of descending the river to sack the little settlement at Montreal. The issue was epic in significance; the background was grand; the incident superbly heroic in quality. The subject might well have been treated in a long narrative, but Lampman preferred to concentrate tightly upon the climactic action and to despatch the whole in just short of a hundred lines. The entire poem cannot be given here: two extracts will show

Lampman's powers in presenting men and their fate with
dramatic intensity and ripe understanding. The first
is his elaborate comparison of the individual hero with a
desperately enduring moose:

Silent, white-faced, again and again,
Charged and hemmed round by furious hands
Each for a moment faces them all and stands
In his little desperate ring; like a tired bull-moose
Whom scores of sleepless wolves, a ravening pack,
Have chased all night, all day
Through the snow-laden woods, like famine let loose;
And he turns at last in his track
Against a wall of rock and stands at bay;
Round him with terrible sinews and teeth of steel
They charge and recharge; but with many a furious plunge and
    wheel,
Hither and thither over the trampled snow
He tosses them bleeding and torn;
Till, driven, and ever to and fro
Harried, wounded and weary grown,
His mighty strength gives way
And all together they fasten upon him and drag him down.

In passing it is worth noting that Lampman's nature poetry
has been of fields and woods and streams, of birds and
insects: here for the first time he deals with one of the great
creatures of the wilds. And throughout the extended image
persistently, almost continuously, the reader is invited to
emotion and thought about man, about the valour, the
endurance, the tragic failure and heroic stature of man.
Nature is a background for man, as it is throughout the
poem. The other extract is the elegiac lyric with which
"At the Long Sault" closes:

All night by the foot of the mountain
    The little town lieth at rest;
The sentries are peacefully pacing;
    And neither from East nor from West

Is there rumour of death or of danger;
    None dreameth tonight in his bed
That ruin was near and the heroes
    That met it and stemmed it are dead.

But afar in the ring of the forest
    Where the air is so tender with May
And the waters are wild in the moonlight,
    They lie in their silence of clay.

The numberless stars out of heaven
    Look down with a pitiful glance;
And the lilies asleep in the forest
    Are closed like the lilies of France.

After the firm, deep sound of the preceding lines, telling of
the heroes' end, the swift, gentle fall of the anapaests
soothes the spirit, and persuades one to believe that the
dark and terrible conflict by the river was no mere explosion
of primitive force, that it was a reassuring act, preserving
serenity and safety for Montreal—for Canada—and encour-
aging us to share that serenity and safety.   But lest we hold
the sacrifice too cheap, the epigrammatic close is there to
remind us of death—but also to suggest resurgence.   It is
a great elegy to be set with Duncan Campbell Scott's "The
Closed Door"; and no one will question that here at least
Lampman shows his power as a poet of human feeling and
action.

"At the Long Sault" gives a measure of the power
Lampman had at the end of his career in dealing with
human themes.   It is not notable in narrative; but the
great virtues of moral poetry are here—the wisdom, the
intensity, the beauty, which all depend in part upon the
awareness that the particular situation, the selected personalities, are parts of a great whole.

VIII

The effect produced by "At the Long Sault" depends
in large measure on the formal resources on which the
poet here draws so happily. To read it convinces us
how sound was Scott's lament that his friend's career "was
cut short just as he was beginning to develop new and freer
forms of expression." We may now look back over his
poetry to inquire where in general its formal beauty lies,
and what formal resources Lampman most often uses.
He is undoubtedly the most pictorial of Canadian poets:
again and again the nature of the Ottawa Valley is seized
with absolute fidelity and with something superior to
fidelity—the painter's insight into the essence of a scene.
"Heat" is a perfect instance of this achievement. Nothing
could be more patiently faithful than:

> On the brook yonder not a breath
> Disturbs the spider or the midge.
> The water-bugs draw close beneath
> The cool gloom of the bridge.

The picture is so clear that anyone who has at midsummer
leaned over a bridge spanning a quiet stream has a reminiscence of recreative vividness, leading him to recall all the
essential circumstances and renewing for him in great
intensity all the main sensations and emotions he experienced and indeed the very "feel" of the remembered
moment, almost in full vigour. Or take the opening lines
of "Winter Evening":

> Tonight the very horses springing by
> Toss gold from whitened nostrils. . . .

for fidelity in a city scene, fidelity irradiated by verbal
magic; and the following lines for picture melting into
suggestion, another of Lampman's chief resources, present
in less degree in the passages already cited:

> In a dream
> The streets that narrow to the westward gleam
> Like rows of golden palaces; and high
> From all the crowded chimneys tower and die
> A thousand aureoles.

In the picture and suggestion of nature—or of the city's charm—lies Lampman's chief formal beauty. Sometimes, as in the lines from "Heat," his manner is bare, sometimes, as in the "Winter Evening," it is luxuriant.

Luxuriant or bare, his manner was always carefully studied. His manuscripts show how laboriously he sought for the exact word or phrase. From thousands of examples I take but three, the first of which will represent his quest of the ideal single word. In the sonnet "At Dusk," he first wrote of

> the night wind
> Wandering in *breaths* from off the darkening hill

and *breaths* gave way to *waves*, then, unfortunately, to *strata*, then to *snatches*, and, finally and happily, to *puffs*. Often the alternatives heap up along the margin and sometimes in inextricable disorder above and below the inadequate word. Note, too, how he reshapes an entire line:

> Where the soft sunshine one long moment more

in "A Sunset at Les Eboulements," becoming more pictorially though less musically—

> Where the long light across the lit sea-floor

and then, with something more of Lampman's magical kind of fidelity,

> The sun's last shaft beyond the gray sea-floor,

Sometimes, but by no means so frequently, a longer passage is fully reconsidered, as in the opening lines of a late sonnet, "The Passing of Spring," which originally ran:

All, all are gone, the first strange flowers; the glow
    Of birthroot in the forest depths away,
    The waxen bloodroot in her suit of grey,
The bridal song of many a bird we know.

Looking critically at this, we can imagine Lampman pausing
over the first line as too crowded, over the repetition in
birthroot and *bloodroot,* and the unsatisfactory contrast
between the mention of specific flowers and the general
allusion to birds.   We can understand his wish to make an
entirely fresh start, drafting the opening thus:

Petal by petal all the flowers that blow
    Loosen and fall and vanish from our ken,
    Till the long-changing year returns again
With other hopes and griefs we do not know.

This is musical; none of the aesthetic problems in the first
draft remains; but all pictorial quality has gone, and from
the outset spring is little more than a psychological state.
Lampman makes another and a final try:

No longer in the meadow coigns shall blow
    The creamy blood-root in her suit of gray,
    But all the first strange flowers have passed away,
Gone with the childlike dreams that touched us so.

The second line comes from the first version, with one
admirable modification, *waxen* becoming *creamy;* the rapid
reference to *strange flowers* is happily expanded; the new
first line, keeping the movement and the rhyming word of
the opening of the second version, supplies a setting for the
bloodroot; and instead of the allusions to the future in that
version there is a pathetically powerful reference to the past,
to the psychological spring.   Music, image and feeling are
all fused, as in neither of the earlier versions.

Intense concern for the word and the phrase is the
outstanding feature of Lampman's corrections in manu-

script. He seldom modifies his main idea; a little more often he substitutes one image for another, as in some of the examples that have been given; most of the time he is in quest of a word or a phrase that is more pictorial or more musical. His verbal sensitiveness recalls that of the English poets whom at his best he most resembles, Keats and Tennyson.

As metrist Lampman is not strikingly inventive. Until his last years all his favoured forms were among those which the experience of others had tried and approved—the sonnet, the rhyming quatrain, the stanzaic forms of Keats's major odes, and a six-line stanza consisting of a quatrain followed by a couplet. In the mid-'nineties he became more experimental, and it is probable that the more unusual stanza forms he then began to use, alternatively with his former preferences, reflect the emotional struggles he was undergoing.

Of these struggles Duncan Campbell Scott has told a little in the preface to the selections from Lampman published in 1925. Scott speaks of "evidences in the poems and the letters of spiritual adventures and perturbations that were not apparent even to the closest companion," and after quoting a few sentences from letters concludes by saying these will "prove the existence but not the plot of an intense personal drama." The period of struggle runs almost from the beginning of the 'nineties to the end of Lampman's life, in 1899; its greatest acuteness may be fixed at about the middle of the period. It was then that he wrote to his friend and fellow-poet, E. W. Thomson, that "I have gone through so much inward trouble that it has somewhat broken me, and I do not take wing, so to speak, very readily"; and again that "to tell the truth I have been under such a heavy strain of feeling during the last year or two that I have come to look on the matter of publishing and fame, etc., as of very little importance at all." What the "plot" of the "intensely personal drama" was has not been disclosed; but it is evident that what occurred was more than a crisis of social pessimism, that the deepest and most secret elements of Lampman's nature were involved.

That such developments should also affect his poetic forms is natural. The very first poem in the *Alcyone* collection, the title piece, is impressively different in form from anything that Lampman had previously done. Its first strophe is sufficient to show the newness of the form:

> In the silent depth of space
> Immeasurably old, immeasurably far,
> Glittering with a silver flame
> Through eternity,
> Rolls a great and burning star,
> With a noble name,
> Alcyone!

The blend of rhyming and unrhyming lines, long lines and short lines, in an irregular pattern is one of Lampman's experiments. Another is the choice of stanza for the "Ode to the Hills," but here the experiment is in greater elaborateness. Still another is the long-lined couplet he uses in the narrative called "The Woodcutter's Hut." None of these experiments is as striking as what Lampman attempted in "At the Long Sault" where, as in "Alcyone," he is undergoing some influence from Duncan Campbell Scott, who had moved much more quickly towards flexibility of form. The formal experiments are too diverse to enable one to predict the sort of verse Lampman would have written had he lived into the new century: their significance is in reflecting the tumult of his spirit.

It may be useful to say something of Lampman's conduct of the sonnet, the form in which he wrote most often and felt that he was at his happiest. He has no constant or usual sonnet-form: sometimes he uses octave and sestet, sometimes he prefers quatrains and couplet; in his octaves he usually has three rhymes (abba acca), although in some of his finest sonnets he restricts himself to the statutory two; he likes to set his couplet between the second and third quatrain, rather than at the close of the poem, but this liking is not consistent. Since he also likes to introduce his sestet with a couplet, the close reader grows to expect that the ninth and tenth lines of a Lampman sonnet—whether in quatrains and couplet or in octave and sestet—will form a rhyming interlude. How successful he is in this little device may be seen in "A Sunset at Les Eboulements," a loosely Italian sonnet:

> Broad shadows fall. On all the mountain side
> The scythe-swept fields are silent. Slowly home
> By the long beach the high-piled hay-carts come,
> Splashing the pale salt shallows. Over wide
> Fawn-coloured wastes of mud the slipping tide,
> Round the dun rocks and wattled fisheries,
> Creeps murmuring in. And now by twos and threes,
> O'er the slow spreading pools with clamorous chide,
> *Belated crows from strip to strip take flight*
> *Soon will the first star shine; yet ere the night*
> Reach onward to the pale green distances,
> The sun's last shaft beyond the gray sea-floor
> Still dreams upon the Kamouraska shore,
> And the long line of golden villages.

The effect in a sonnet consisting of quatrains and couplet can be seen in the admirable "On Lake Temiscamingue":

> A single dreamy elm, that stands between
>   The sombre forest and the wan-lit lake,
> Halves with its slim grey stem and pendent green
>   The shadowed point. Beyond it without break
> Bold brows of pine-topped granite bend away,
>   Far to the southward, fading off in grand
> Soft folds of looming purple. Cool and gray,

The point runs out, a blade of thinnest sand.
Two rivers meet beyond it: wild and clear,
  The deepening thunder breaks upon the ear—
The one descending from its forest home
  By many an eddied pool and murmuring fall—
The other cloven through the mountain wall,
  A race of tumbled rocks, a roar of foam.

With these illustrations of one little refinement in the oldest of the forms he was accustomed to use, we may take leave of Lampman's art, the most careful that any Canadian has yet exhibited in verse—or in prose.

IX

It remains to inquire whether Lampman's reputation at home or abroad is in keeping with his deserts. At home, as I have said, his is the first place. At Morpeth, in south-western Ontario, a cairn commemorates his birth: it was unveiled with impressive ceremony in which men of letters, educators and plain citizens confirmed the praise so eloquently expressed by Duncan Campbell Scott. In the capital, where he lived, the municipal library long ago installed a window in which Lampman's head appears beside those of the major poets of England. The selected edition of 1925 remains in print; and the collected works as well as the volumes that appeared in his lifetime are sought by bibliophiles and patriots. No poems from our nineteenth century are so widely known and quoted, often by quite unliterary people, as some of his sonnets. The man is admired for the gentle firmness of his character. Much, very much, of Lampman's reputation has come from the admirable fashion in which his friend Scott conceived and carried out the duties of literary executor, never missing an appropriate occasion to impress upon his countrymen the quality of the man and his work. Forty-five years have

passed since Lampman wrote his last sonnet and set below
it a single line from the *Odyssey*, which may be translated:
"For men age quickly in evil fortune"; but in his own
country the fortune of the poetry written in such privation
and pain has been good, not evil, for he has the rare fortune
to be acceptable to a new impatient generation.   Abroad
he is today unknown.   The charm and fidelity of his nature
poetry must always be more intimately moving to those
who know the Canadian seasons, the beauty of sunlight
upon the pure, deep snow and the even greater beauty of
sunrise and sunset, the quick greenness of the Canadian
spring, the northern lakes a cold blue at the height of
summer, the violent colours of the fall.   But this poetry,
and the finest of his lyrical cries, the wisest of his sonnets,
the recovered "At the Long Sault," have only to be known
to be valued.   Lampman's voice is too genuine to be
ignored for ever in any country where the language he
used with such patient and suggestive fidelity is the
language men speak.

2. DUNCAN CAMPBELL SCOTT

I

IN 1924 Archibald MacMechan, who was then nearing
the end of a long career as professor of English literature at
Dalhousie University, brought out his *Headwaters of Canadian Literature*.   The fruit of a course given for many years,
this is the most distinguished and sensible book about the
national literature yet written by an English-speaking
Canadian.   "It is," he says in his preface, "emphatically
a sketch"; and on the first page of the copy I possess the
warning not to expect too much is repeated in MacMechan's
elegant Victorian hand.   What he meant was that he

preferred to keep his two hundred and thirty small pages
for the major figures, to speak of the lesser worthies only
when their work had shaped the development of letters
or culture.   Still, MacMechan's standards are not rigorous;
space is found to refer to more than forty poets and to
study with care some dozen of these.   Duncan Campbell
Scott is not of the dozen; he is not even of the forty.   The
only allusion to him is the mention in passing that he had
written the life of a governor of the ancient Province of
Upper Canada.   When MacMechan wrote, Scott's first
collection had been before the public for more than thirty
years; half a dozen others had followed it; and Scott's
productive career was indeed approaching its end.

How is such an omission to be explained?   It was
assuredly not the result of any personal spite—it simply
reflects the long failure of the Canadian public and Canadian
critics to do anything like justice to Scott's powers.   For
justice he has had to wait much longer than any of the other
poets of his generation.   Carman and Roberts and even
minòr figures such as Wilfred Campbell and Tom MacInnes
were legends in their prime; in varying ways they embodied
what the public expected a lyrical poet to be.   On whatever
they did, wherever they went—and they all wandered and
turned their hands to many things—they printed the mark
of a peculiar personality, self-centred and striking.   On
the surface Scott has lived the life of a devoted and successful civil servant; he has been little known outside Ottawa
except among professional associates; even where he has
been known, the shyness and austerity which have marked
his relations with all but his intimates have left a colourless
impression; if those he met casually were aware that he
wrote verses, such a relaxation seemed to them somewhat
out of character.   Lampman, no less shy and no less bound
to a narrow circle, had no substantial fame till his early
death made of him what he has remained—our Canadian
symbol of the fragile artist worn down by the rigours of our

climate and our social and economic structure. The effect of personal impressions does not, however, suffice to explain the disparity between the earlier reputation of Scott and that of his contemporaries. There are other reasons why Canadians say in one breath—and even today: "Lampman, Carman and Roberts," and only after a marked pause: "Oh, and Duncan Campbell Scott, too." It is to be remembered that Roberts gave the lead to the group, and that his mellow classical pieces mingling myth and landscape, and his homely local pictures, fixed for the time what the range of Canadian poetry was to be. "When I was beginning to write," he remarked in a recent letter, "I was not aware of any such thing as Canadian literature. . . . But I did dream of *starting* a *Canadian* literature; and I joyously hailed the first efforts of Lampman and Carman, as the beginnings of it." The reminiscence is exceedingly revealing. Roberts set the course and warmly welcomed those who rivalled him, recognizing especially the values in Lampman and Carman. Lampman appreciated his debt to Roberts at its full size: in the chapter on his poetry I have quoted his enthusiastic response to the first of Roberts's collections. His awareness of obligation was matched by Carman's. The three of them, whatever their differences in temperament, were drawn to many of the same kinds of subjects and to forms if not the same at least closely akin. Where one was known and approved, the others needed only to be known to be approved also. Scott was never to be wholly at home in their world, no matter how he might try to write in their fashion, no matter how well he might come to know them—and he was to become one of Lampman's closest intimates. In a word, it is Scott's originality which explains the long time he had to wait before readers in any considerable numbers began to appreciate that he was one of the chief masters of Canadian literature.

II

Scott was Ottawa-born and if he was not Ottawa-bred he returned to the city when he was sixteen, and it has since been his home.   He grew to maturity in the shadow of Parliament, and his imagination was early caught by the capital.   "The city of the end of things," Lampman was to call it in one of those moments when he ceased to dream of its towers and hills and sunsets; for Scott it has always been the "maiden queen of all the towered towns."   As a small child he was taken to hear Joseph Howe speak in the Commons; he was appointed to the civil service as early as 1879 after an interview with Sir John A. Macdonald; into his idea of Ottawa and of Canada there has always entered that stamp of greatness that the Fathers of Confederation could give, and none of them so imaginatively and vividly as the Nova Scotian man of letters who was our most culti-vated statesman and the Ontario strategist and dreamer who was our most far-sighted founder.   As well as a pro-vincial town where the currents of world thought, art and action arrived with extreme slowness—this was how Lamp-man judged it—Scott saw in Ottawa something to stimu-late the imagination and thrill the spirit.   As he wrote in one of his earliest poems:

> Fair as a shrine that makes
> The wonder of a dream, imperious towers
> Pierce and possess the sky, guarding the halls
> Where our young strength is welded strenuously;
> While in the East the star of morning dowers
> The land with a large tremulous light, that falls
> A pledge and presage of our destiny.

It was natural that he should decide on a career in the civil service; and at eighteen, without going to college, he entered the Department of Indian Affairs.   He was not then conscious of any poetic impulse: his aesthetic expression

was then in music. Only after Lampman had come to
Ottawa in 1883, and become a friend, did Scott think of
writing verse. That splendid May morning two years
before when Lampman had read Roberts in the meadow at
Trinity College was the beginning not of one but of two
poetic careers. Scott wrote slowly and critically; but before
the 'eighties ended his verses in magazines were attracting
notice, and when in 1889 W. D. Lighthall published his
important anthology, *Songs of the Great Dominion*, Scott's
verse was represented.

III

In 1893, just after he had passed his thirtieth year, he
brought out his first collection, *The Magic House and Other
Poems*. In that same year Carman's first collection
appeared, with its famous title piece, *Low Tide on Grand
Pré*. Carman, as has been suggested, began his career
with subjects and tones which strongly recalled Lampman
and Roberts, both of whom had established themselves with
the Canadian readers of verses some years earlier. Before
four months had passed, Carman's book was in its second
edition; Scott, more original, was not to be so fortunate.

In his work, it is so even in this first collection, there
is a mixture of restraint and intensity which grasps at one
and will not let one go. As one reads the collection through
today, it is to be struck by the predominance of the dark
and the powerful—night, storm, the wilderness, the angry
sea. The nature he depicts and evokes is a harsh and
violent nature:

> . . . a land that man has not sullied with his intrusion
> When the aboriginal shy dwellers in the broad solitudes
> Are asleep in their innumerable dens and night haunts
> Amid the dry ferns.

His strongest pictures of this Nature come from later collections—the lines that have been quoted belong to a poem that appeared as late as 1916—and it is when these are reached that an attempt may best be made to define Scott's view of the external world. Here it need only be said that Lampman, Carman and Roberts have in the main presented the more or less cultivated parts of Canada, or those marginal to settlement, Scott, above all those that are untouched or scarcely touched by the hand of man, for example, "the lonely loon-haunted Nipigon reaches" and "the enormous targe of Hudson Bay." By his choice of the wilds he has won an immense advantage over his contemporaries. They usually write of Canada—and this appears in their images and rhythms as well as in their substance—as if it were a large English county, and it is hard for them to convey in their nature-verse any feeling which has not been more powerfully presented by one or another of the English poets. Imitation almost imposes itself upon them. The path to originality is wide before Scott. His problem is to find a form suitable and adequate for his novel matter. It will not be supposed that he succeeded in finding that form at the very outset of his career.

Indeed, the nature-pieces in his first collection are not as satisfying as the dream-pieces. These are definitely *fin de siècle*. They introduce one to a nightmarish world, in which not only are logical relations suspended as they are in symbolist verse, in much of Carman's early work to take a Canadian example, but the relation even between images is extremely loose, exactly as in vivid dreams. The quality of Scott's dream-pieces has been perfectly caught in John Masefield's tribute to one of them, "The Piper of Arll," which in 1895 quickened his interest in poetry when he was a factory-hand at Yonkers:

This was the first poem by a living writer to touch me to the quick. It was narrative; it was delicate phantasy; it was about the sea and singing and a romantic end.   I did not know it at the time but it was a choice example of the work of the romantic poets of that decade.   Its longing, its wistfulness, and the perfection of some of its images made deep impressions upon me. . . .   Years later I came upon the writing of a critic [William Archer] who mentions it as a poem "the symbolism of which escapes me."   Well, let it escape.   The romantic mood and the dream may be of deep personal significance and joy, even if the author's thought eludes us.

In general, even in "The Piper of Arll," the thought does not elude, but is a mass of suggestions which do indeed lack definiteness.   The two sonnets which are grouped under the caption "In the House of Dreams" might have come from *The Yellow Book:* in them we find a lady, a blade of gladiolus, a fountain, a serpent, a crow and finally a "little naked lad." Even a casual reading conveys the general sense of love as a source of pain coming into a bower of beauty in which some ugly elements have been awaiting its advent in order to coalesce.   A careful reading does not do much more to clarify the sense: but we are not eluded, we are merely held in an atmosphere heavy with suggestion.   The title-piece is similar in effect, harking back to the Pre-Raphaelite mood as much *fin de siècle* poetry did: the woman in the magic house is a sister of the Blessed Damozel and of the Lady of Shalott.   The movement has the hushed and halting quality that is found in much of the early work of William Morris.   Where outside Morris has his movement been so perfectly achieved as in such a stanza as this:

> But no thing shall habit there,
>   There no human foot shall fall,
> No sweet word the silence stir,
>   Naught her name shall call,
> Nothing come to comfort her.

There is possibly a brusqueness in the fourth line which is not Morris's, and which, recurring throughout the poem, gives a strangely powerful effect as it punctually comes to break the dream-movement. Original, too, but quite in Morris's manner is the internal rhyme in the fifth line, another designed and repeated effect. What is more significant from the present point of view is the absence of perspective: everything is on the same level, the size of things and their demands upon our attention do not vary. Nothing can better achieve the effect of dream than this primitively unorganized succession of imagery. At the end of the piece, although it is evident that the woman passed through a variety of states, one does not know where the turning point, or turning points, lay. Just what these states were does not greatly matter; nor does it greatly matter how she passed from one to another; what does matter is a diffused sense of agonies undergone in silence. The reader feels dimly oppressed—an effect of restrained intensity.

Restrained intensity is also sought in a very simple narrative, one of Scott's very earliest compositions, called "At the Cedars," something miles removed from the kind of verse that has just been considered. This is a narrative essentially akin to his prose tales, and especially to the mysterious tale of the mythical lumberman, Welly Legrand. It tells of a log-jam on the Ottawa, in which a man is caught and killed in the presence of his girl, who set out for the jam in a canoe only to be caught and killed as quickly and brutally as her lover. What I mean by an attempt at restrained intensity of manner will be evident from so brief a passage as this, especially from its laconic close:

> He went up like a block
> With the shock,
> And when he was there
> In the air,

> Kissed his hand
> To the land;
> When he dropped
> My heart stopped,
> For the first logs had caught him
> And crushed him;
> When he rose in his place
> There was blood on his face.

It is significant that in such a subject, new to Scott and treated in such a bald and simple fashion, the same fundamental quality is evident. It is significant because it appears to point to something permanent and instinctive in his practice, permanent and instinctive in himself. We shall see that the appearance is not deceptive.

IV

A search for the adequate theme and the adequate form in which restrained intensity may express itself—here is the emotional centre of Scott's work. In the two collections that followed his first, *Labour and the Angel* (1898) and *New World Lyrics and Ballads* (1905), there are many failures and a larger number of approaches to success. Most of the failures are similar in theme and form to poems that were being written by the general run of Scott's contemporaries in Canada and in the United States. It was an age in which only bold experimenters and original temperaments went beyond the gentle feeling, the gentle word, the gentle landscape. In exasperation Edwin Arlington Robinson was pleading:

> Oh for a poet—for a beacon bright
> To rift this changeless glimmer of dead gray;
> To spirit back the Muses, long astray,
> And flush Parnassus with a newer light;

> To put these little sonnet-men to flight
> Who fashion in a shrewd mechanic way,
> Songs without souls that flicker for a day,
> To vanish in irrevocable night.

In Canada there was less of the shrewd mechanic, less of the sonneteering, but just as much of the dead gray. Scott took the infection. When he wrote in the gentle manner he was not as winning, because not as genuine, as Lampman or Carman: it was not his manner and he wrote in it only because he was not yet in sure possession of a manner of his own, and highly sensitive to the winds of taste.

It will be more interesting to consider the approaches to success, in which there is something more original. Sometimes he hits upon a theme which is proper to him, but is impeded by his choice of form. A striking instance is his "Mission of the Trees," a narrative of two Indians, father and son, the only Christians in their settlement; the son, about to die, pleads with his father to take him to the Christian mission; setting out in midwinter, the father collapses and dies, beside the corpse of the son, frozen in the drifts. All the intensity Scott might desire is in this theme: intensity of effort, intensity of conflict between man and nature. But Scott wished not only to be intense, but also to establish restraint—he was determined not to overdo his effect. The result was too quiet a note. Set side by side with the primitive and violent materials that have been mentioned, such images as these:

> Never
> Bell-note sounded so forlorn,
> Like a plover in the clearing
> When the frost is on the corn

or

> Then the cloud was spent at midnight
> And the world so gleamed with snow,
> That the frosty moon looked downward
> On a moon that glowed below

delicately Tennysonian, and with a liquidity and regularity of rhythm that has nothing whatever in common with the bitterness of the experiences to which they relate. How can one explain the amazing discrepancy between form and substance? The substance was to give the intensity, the form the restraint. Scott was here satisfied with a balance that is mechanical, a balance that was achieved by setting two entities side by side and making sure that they had the same weight. For the greatest effects the balance must be organic: the intensity and the restraint must fuse. This they do not often do in Scott's early or intermediate volumes.

When they do his poetry is not to be equalled, I think, by any of the Canadian poets of his generation. "The Forsaken," another Indian narrative, is an admirable example of his success. In this piece he presents two pictures. The first gives us a young squaw with her papoose, caught in a snowstorm on a frozen northern lake; to save her child from death she breaks a hole in the ice and tries to hook a fish; she is without success till she baits the hook with her own flesh; strengthened by food, she is able to give milk and keep her baby living till she can rejoin her people. In the second picture an Indian family, in which this same squaw is now the withered grandmother, reaches, as winter approaches, the same spot where she had so long ago baited her hook; the rest of the group sneak off across the lake, leaving the old woman behind. The poem is impressive in many ways, but what now concerns us is its fundamental quality, its perfect fusion of intensity and restraint.

Let us look back for a moment to that earlier narrative, "At the Cedars," which presents the death of two lovers in a log jam. "At the Cedars" is an undoubted success; indeed, I think it is the best narrative Scott wrote before "The Forsaken." It is not usually fair to estimate the quality of a narrative poem by that of a few lines, however good; the effect of narrative poetry, even more than that of other kinds of poetry, is a total effect.   When a short passage of narrative is abstracted from its context it will often seem rough and even commonplace, as well as false in tone.   With this in mind to preserve us from making too harsh a judgment, let us look at the lines from "At the Cedars" which have already been quoted.   Do not such lines as:

> When he dropped
> My heart stopped

fall short of the tragic note such a poem should sustain, fall short because they are a little over-sharp, and over-tense? The reading of the whole poem would confirm such a criticism.   Here and there it verges on melodrama, intensity without restraint.   The first of the pictures in "The Forsaken" is given in short lines, but it leaves an effect not of sharpness but of lucidity and firmness.   This is partly because the lines are unrhymed, but the absence of rhyme is not really a cause but merely a concurrent effect of a difference in mood.   What this mood is becomes more evident in the second picture, where the lines lengthen and the note deepens.   Set beside the description of the crisis in "At the Cedars," this account of the state of mind of the old woman as she appreciates that she has been forsaken:

> Then, without a sigh,
> Valiant, unshaken,
> She smoothed her dark locks under her kerchief,
> Composed her shawl in state,
> Then folded her hands ridged with sinews and corded with veins,
> Folded them across her breasts spent with the nourishing of children
> Gazed at the sky past the tops of the cedars. . . .

Here at last is the magical union towards which Scott had
so long been moving.

V

Not a few of the poems in which he achieves this
peculiar kind of perfection have to do with the Indians.
Of all Canadian poets, indeed of all Canadian imaginative
writers, he has best succeeded in making great literature
out of such distinctively Canadian material as our aborigines
supply.   This is wholly fitting.   The entire professional
career of Duncan Campbell Scott was passed in the federal
Department of Indian Affairs in which he rose, while still
young, to be Deputy Superintendent General, a post which
he held for about twenty years.*   During that period, and
indeed for some time before his formal accession to the
post, he was the chief moulder of departmental policy, an
administrator of rare imaginative sympathy and almost
perfect wisdom.   He was never the *rond de cuir:* he was
always eager to see his charges, and especially in his later
years in the department when he had greater freedom of
movement was much among them, both on the reservations
and in the wild and remote areas where the Indians continue
to lead a life which preserves much of the nomadic and
picturesque quality of the past.   He was led to the conclusion, significant not only for his policies but for his
poetry, that Indians are primarily to be understood as men
and women, not as creatures of a different race and colour
from ours.   His poetry presents them not as noble savages,
whose emotions run in courses unknown to us, surprising

*I append a list of the main stages in his progress through the depart-
ment of Indian Affairs: Clerk, with various grades (1879-1896); Secretary
of the Department (1896-1905); Chief Clerk and Accountant (1905-1909);
Superintendent of Indian Education (1909-1913); Deputy Superintendent
General of Indian Affairs (1913-1932).   The deputy superintendency general
is the highest civil-service post in the department; the superintendency general
is vested in a member of the Dominion cabinet.

us by their strangeness, but as complex yet intelligible persons. What is the real theme of "The Forsaken"? It is nothing less than a universal tragedy, the tragedy of Lear and Goriot. Those who once were strong become weak; their value dwindles and those whom they reared from helpless weakness to strength discard them as costly superfluities.

The same universality marks another of the Indian poems of his middle period, that sonnet of rare beauty, "The Onondaga Madonna." Here the theme is the tragic confusion of the *métis*, and nowhere in his work does Scott show a more delicate imaginative sympathy than in his dealings with those of mixed blood. The sonnet ends:

> And closer in the shawl about her breast,
> The latest promise of her nation's doom,
> Paler than she her baby clings and lies,
> The primal warrior gleaming from his eyes;
> He sulks, and burdened with his infant gloom,
> He draws his heavy brows and will not rest.

Here what shines out from the quiet lines is not the specific tragedy of a European-Indian mixture, but the general tragedy of all blood-mixture. It is the same with the longer, no less powerful and scarcely less finished "The Half Breed Girl." The degree to which Scott universalizes his Indian characters may be suggested, perhaps, by an error into which I was led by the poem "Night Burial in the Forest" and by his comment upon the error. Here he tells of a sordid love set against the awful background of the untouched wilderness. One man kills another because of a fancy for a cheap girl, and the murderer rushes off to vanish into the north. The evocation of the dark forests on the river bank, and the flare of torches in the little camp at the water's edge, led me to imagine that the poem had to do with Indians. Scott has told me that I was wrong, and that he had in mind an expedition of lumberjacks along the Nipigon, but he added that the slip was "unimportant": to him lumberjack and Indian are of the same stuff.

Throughout almost all of the Indian poems the fusion of intensity and restraint is notable. It comes to its perfection in a piece longer than any that have been mentioned, "Powassan's Drum." To the end of a poem almost one hundred and fifty lines in length, Scott maintains his spell. There is no monotony of effect. The poem begins quietly. At a safe psychological distance, as vagrant tourists, we watch the old medicine man, Powassan, beating his drum with a fierce steadiness; he impresses us with just the idle curiosity that any anachronism might provoke. Slowly the drum begins to drown all other impressions; from our safe distance we have been pulled within the range where the beat seems to be nothing short of the "pulse of Being"; we cannot remember a time when the beat did not dominate our world or conceive a time when it will not. Everything has been poisoned: air, earth and water repeat the appalling sound. Our senses play us false, and Scott suggests our corrupted state by a weird and fully suitable image:

> Then from the reeds stealing,
> A shadow noiseless,
> A canoe moves noiseless as sleep,
> Noiseless as the trance of deep sleep
> And an Indian still as a statue,
> Molded out of deep sleep,
> Headless, still as a headless statue
> Molded out of deep sleep,
> Sits modelled in full power,
> Haughty in manful power,
> Headless and impotent in power.
> The canoe stealthy as death
> Drifts to the throbbing of Powassan's Drum.

Here by his rhythm, Scott has lulled the critical powers and
we easily make the final step in the long process which began
as we stood in curiosity outside Powassan's tent and which
ends with our immersion in a world of being that normally
would have no meaning for us, but now takes on a huge and
sinister suggestion.   The outlines become clearer, and the
rhythms less incantatory as the passage continues:

> The Indian fixed like bronze
> Trails his severed head
> Through the dead water
> Holding it by the hair,
> By the plaits of hair,
> Wound with sweet grass and tags of silver.
> The face looks through the water
> Up to its throne on the shoulders of power,
> Unquenched eyes burning in the water,
> Piercing beyond the shoulders of power
> Up to the fingers of the storm cloud.

The threatening beat is sharply broken at the close of the
poem: a storm breaks upon the world, and at its climax
seems like the prolongation of the beat of Powassan's drum.

The height of Scott's power in dealing with Indian
material is reached in this poem and in a much quieter piece,
a poem within a poem, the lines on the death of Akoose
which form a brief passage in the "Lines in Memory of
Edmund Morris."   Something of the power in the Akoose
passage derives from its very carefully established relation
with its setting.   Morris, a painter who was an intimate of
Scott's, died suddenly at a time when the poet was intending
to reply to his last letter; even though his friend is dead
Scott finds himself eager to answer, and at the beginning of
the piece presents himself as pondering over the characteristic illegibilities in Morris's letter:

> I gather from the writing,
> The coin that you had flipt,
> Turned tails; and so you compel me
> To meet you at Touchwood Hills:
> Or, mayhap, you are trying to tell me
> The sum of a painter's ills:
> Is that Phimister Proctor
> Or something about a doctor?
> Well, nobody knows, but Eddie,
> Whatever it is, I'm ready.

In this jaunty quasi-doggerel, Scott sets out on his composition.   As he recalls their expeditions into the wilds the note becomes graver and some quiet, suggestive nature verse follows; from the wilds Scott passes smoothly and in an easier vein to their human equivalents, the Indians. Picture follows picture, accurate and evocative, many of them presented in language as easy as the opening of the poem:

> And well I recall the weirdness
> Of that evening at Qu'Appelle,
> In the wigwam with old Sakimay,
> The keen, acrid smell
> As the kinnikinick was burning;
> The planets outside were turning,
> And the little splints of poplar
> Flared with a thin, gold flame.

The verses lengthen and deepen as Scott turns to meditation, slowly convincing himself that human life records more good than ill, that the victories of man, indecisive as they are, are yet more substantial than his defeats.   Persistence, he concludes,

> Persistence is the master of this life;
> The master of these little lives of ours;
> To the end—effort—even beyond the end.

There is the bare statement, lent a mild glory by the cadence of the verse.   Akoose shall serve as its illustration: forty lines, just preceding the end of the poem, which exceeds two hundred and fifty, demonstrate that for Scott the poetic mode of thought is more congenial than the rhetorical, that after the statement, fine as it is, must come the suggestion, the persuasive individual case.

The opening lines are strong and heavy:

> Think of the death of Akoose, fleet of foot,
> Who, in his prime, a herd of antelope
> From sunrise, without rest, a hundred miles
> Drove through rank prairie, loping like a wolf,
> Tired them and slew them, ere the sun went down.

With this picture is contrasted, as in "The Forsaken," the humiliating and shameful weakness of old age:

> Akoose, in his old age, blind from the smoke
> Of tepees and the sharp snow light, alone
> With his great-grandchildren, withered and spent,
> Crept in the warm sun along a rope
> Stretched for his guidance.

But the death of Akoose is to be a prouder one than that of the old squaw in "The Forsaken": all she could do was to oppose to the cruelties of nature and of her family an uncomplaining pensive firmness, which, if it had a dignity of its own, was at least as pathetic as it was heroic.   Akoose will act; he seizes a pony that wanders within range and makes off northward to slip down at sunset and lie waiting for death, passive as befits age, but in conditions he has chosen—at the scene of his most brilliant exploit.   Persistence!   *Ewig, ewig, usque ad finem!* as Stein's formula runs in *Lord Jim;* the relation of the incident to the idea is not laboured, but it is clear.

Note how Scott's verse, so varied in this poem, swells and grows richer as he approaches the conclusion:

> There Akoose lay, silent amid the bracken,
> Gathered at last with the Algonquin Chieftains.
> Then the tenebrous sunset was blown out,
> And all the smoky gold turned into cloud wrack.
> Akoose slept forever amid the poplars,
> Swathed by the wind from the far-off Red Deer
> Where dinosaurs sleep, clamped in their rocky tombs.

Even without that last line the death of Akoose has been lifted high above pathos; the old man who crept along the rope to sun himself had given way to the essential form of Akoose, the idea, the fleet and bold chief. All discord had been resolved: the close was adequate to record the death of a hero when that death was a quiet one. The last line adds another effect, congruent with this but surpassing it: Akoose enters into the process of the centuries and his life and death fall into place as parts of a great and ultimately satisfying panorama, which is suddenly given a focus. The incident here reveals its full illustrative value on a high level. Five lines follow to dwell on this and to enforce it:

> Who shall count the time that lies between
> The sleep of Akoose and the dinosaurs?
> Innumerable time, that yet is like the breath
> Of the long wind that creeps upon the prairie
> And dies away with the shadows at sundown.

It remains for Scott to return to his main theme and relate the death of Akoose to the death of Edmund Morris; as he does so he retains the slow, heavy cadence of those last lines.

VI

The perfection of his best Indian pieces is matched in his best nature-verse, and seldom anywhere else in his work. It is in the collections of his middle years that Scott's nature-verse is most fully successful. Many of the poems in *Via Borealis* relate to a canoe-trip which Scott took, in 1906, with his lifelong friend, the eminent critic, Pelham Edgar. In the rocky wilderness of northern Ontario Scott responds to nature, not to the quiet, quasi-maternal being that Lampman sought in his wanderings on the outskirts of Ottawa, but to "quintessential passion."   Where so many more commonplace minds, poets or painters, have felt the nature of our Laurentian shield as silence and repose Scott has found in a multitude of its explicit or suggested activities an enormous intensity—in the loud beat of partridge wings, the wild laughter of loons, the violent colours of sunrise and sunset and their scarcely less violent reflection in the lakes, the exciting maze of fireflies whose trajectories cross and recross, and, most vivid, perhaps, of all his pictures:

> the fatal shore
> Where a bush fire, smouldering, with sudden roar
> Leaped on a cedar and smothered it with light
> And terror. It had left the portage height
> A tangle of slanted spruces burned to the roots,
> Covered still with patches of bright fire.

Scott does not seem to reach to the very heart of the Laurentian intensity as two or three of our painters, notably Tom Thomson, have done.   For him it is only the mass of surface aspects that is violent.   But how violent the surface is! So violent that in "Spring on Mattagami"—a poem for which he himself does not much care—with perfect appropriateness the response to nature is fused with an intensity of sexual feeling not elsewhere to be found in his work. It is worth noting that this poem is modelled closely and carefully on Meredith's "Love in the Valley." It seems wholly in keeping that he should pass from stanzas which smoulder with the colours and scents of the landscape to stanzas which flame with his longing for some ideal woman, whom he pictures in the midst of wild nature, drawing from it a liberation from her hesitations so that she yields to his passion.

Scott's nature-verse was never superior to the effects he produces in some parts of this poem or in the more philosophic "Height of Land," a somewhat later poem from which the image of the bush-fire comes. To some it may appear that "Spring on Mattagami," like some of Scott's first nature-poems, is a juxtaposition rather than a fusion of intensity and restraint. The poem is elaborate and it is slow, but the lines have a fluidity which to my feeling produces fusion: it offers a steady current of emotion with sudden bursts of passion and gradual returns to the more usual pace. It is important to recognize that though the bursts are sudden the returns are graduated, and thus there is no effect of sharp recoil produced by these. Fine as Scott's presentation of nature as passion may be, he would not be a part of the Canadian tradition if he were not more at ease in the presentation he offers in "The Height of Land," where nature is less primitive and more complex. Here, again, he goes beyond the conception of nature as a quasi-maternal being, but his advance is in another direction. In "Spring on Mattagami" he did not appear aware of calm as an aspect of nature: he excluded it. In "The Height of Land" he includes it in a broader conception. "Here," he says, "is peace"; but he goes on to say:

> That Something comes by flashes
> Deeper than peace,—a spell
> Golden and inappellable
> That gives the inarticulate part

Of our strange being one moment of release
That seems more native than the touch of time,
And we must answer in chime;
Though yet no man may tell
The secret of that spell
Golden and inappellable.

The voice in the earlier lines of the passage is the voice of
Wordsworth, but the mind that it expresses is more
modern, more sceptical: it is the mind of Arnold, whom the
later lines suggest in diction and movement as well as idea.
Even Arnold was not so dubious as Scott here shows himself
in his formulation of the Being that lies within nature and
lends to it its deepest meaning.   This Something is neither
calm nor violence.   As the poem proceeds Scott finds
difficulty in maintaining in fusion elements of calm and
elements of something else which is more intense.   He
descends to a historical interpretation, in which he is concerned not with defining the substance of the Something
but with recording the visions of it that men may have.
He suggests that in our time, the ending period of the
"Christ age," the inmost principle of the universe is defined
as love, a love presented rather sketchily as serene and also
passionate; and he conceives a coming age in which the
interpretive power of man will have been extended—there
is no rejection of the idea of the Christ-age but, as before,
an inclusion of one set of ideas in another which is more
comprehensive and more profound.   In the coming age
that Something will receive clearer definition.   But in a
final note of complexity Scott suggests that perhaps there
will never be deeper wisdom, never fuller understanding of
the Something than appears in the summary intuition
described in the passage quoted.   It is one of Scott's
greatest accomplishments to have remained sensitive to all
his intellectual scruples, to have continued a modern man,

and yet to have written, in this poem, with an intensity and depth of emotion which is normally the privilege of assured faith.

VII

The dialectical habit of thought which added a note of distinction to "The Height of Land" is a characteristic in many of Scott's later poems. A curious and powerful instance of dialectical thinking which is also highly poetical is the "Variations on a Seventeenth Century Theme," in the collection of 1921. The theme comes from Henry Vaughan:

> It was high spring, and all the way
> Primrosed, and hung with shade.

Scott's imagination was stimulated by the odd coupling of the primrose and shadow, the symbol of spring and gaiety and love set beside the symbol of death and gloom. Where Milton had written two contrasted poems, each fully working out one-half of the substance here combined, Scott weaves the two halves through a sequence of ten lyrics and meditations. In one Eve takes the primrose with her into outer darkness; in another the path of gaiety and love shifts into the primrose path to the everlasting bonfire; in another, as pure a song as Scott has written, the permanency of a love is presented in terms of a beginning in the primrose light of dawn and an ending only with the final fall of night. The term "variations" suggests very clearly how it is that Scott has turned a method of thought into a poetic approach to life: the analogy with music is evident. As he opens the last of the sequence, he confesses:

> A few chords now for a brimming close,
> No climax, but a fading away
> Into something either grave or gay
> As the line wanders and falters.

But the confession is not to be taken literally; in this final poem the architecture is very careful—it comes to crown the whole. The "Variations" put us in touch with a mind with a rich sense of the diversity of experience and with a power to sort it into emotionally significant categories.

In the outstanding Indian poem of his last collection, the piece called "A Scene at Lake Manitou," the dialectical method is used without musical function. An old squaw carries out all the observances of Christian piety as her son lies dying; when they fail to propitiate she reverts to her tribal gods and, as a sacrifice, begins to hurl into the lake all her treasures. Following his death her thoughts, after sharp oscillations, come to rest slowly in a perfect balance:

> He had gone to his father
> To hunt in the Spirit Land
> And to be with Jesus and Mary.

The effect of this method, whether it is a conspicuous feature of poetic structure as in the "Variations," or simply an approach to experience as here and in "The Height of Land," is to communicate a breadth and depth to the poetry. It is to be admitted, however, that in the dialectical pieces and passages there is less of the restrained intensity than in such a poem as "Powassan's Drum." It is not easy, if it is possible at all, to be at once dialectical and intense, since one cannot be dialectical and simple.

As a purely simple poet Scott has notable powers, powers that have not appeared adequately in this study. One has only to think of his elegy for his daughter, "The Closed Door," with its magic opening:

> The dew falls and the stars fall,
> The sun falls in the west

and after a dozen rich, slow lines reaching its magical close:

> While the sun falls in the west,
> The dew falls and the stars fall.

In its almost perfect simplicity—there is but one dissonant
note, a single word, "caressed"—it is one of the best
fusions of restraint and intensity in Scott's work. Beside
it may be set, without fear, the hymn he wrote during the
first world war, the hymn that begins:

> Those we have loved the dearest,
> The bravest and the best. . . .

At least I believe this may be set beside the more personal
elegy, but it is inseparable in my memory from an evening
I spent with Scott.

It was one of the many evenings in the summer of 1942
when I talked with him in the huge, high-ceilinged room at
the back of his rambling house. Along the walls were low
bookcases filled, for the most part, with first editions and
the collected works of modern poets; on top of them were
varied mementoes of his contacts with the Indians; and
above were the brilliant landscapes of Milne, Emily Carr
and the "Seven," one of the most distinguished small
collections of Canadian painting. Scott took down bat-
tered old volumes of early Canadian poets, of Heavysege,
Sangster and Cameron; he spoke of his arduous canoe trips
long ago up the Nipigon and along Achigan, and of his
memories of London and Florence; he evoked for me the
long sessions in the 'eighties and 'nineties when he and
Lampman, "poor Archie," were forging their poetics; he
told of the welcome he gave to the early work of Marjorie
Pickthall, and of Rupert Brooke's visit to him just before
the last war; he sought to make clear the change in the fibre
of human nature that has occurred in the past half century;
he gave to me the manuscript of one of Lampman's lyrics
and allowed himself to be led on to read a few of his own
briefer pieces, among them the hymn I have quoted from,
which interested him by its resemblance to something he
was just then composing. It was only a week before his
eightieth birthday; the grave, gentle voice was that of an

old man, but what he had to say reflected not old age but exquisite maturity. Here, I thought, as Pater presents Marius thinking of Fronto, was "the one instance" I had seen "of a perfectly tolerable, perfectly beautiful old age— an old age in which there seemed . . . nothing to be regretted, nothing really lost in what the years had taken away. The wise old man . . . would seem to have replaced carefully and consciously each natural trait of youth, as it departed from him, by an equivalent grace of culture."

3. E. J. PRATT

I

ORIGINALITY has been rare in Canadian literature, and what originality there has been is narrowly limited. In the early generations with whom imaginative writing began, there was a tendency, natural enough in transplanted Englishmen and Americans, to depend on English and American authors for tragedy and comedy, general history and general criticism, philosophical reflection whether in prose or verse, in short for the presentation of all general problems of human experience. Canadians were impelled to write descriptions either of the landscape round about them or of the peculiar circumstances in which they lived: these they must describe for themselves since the material was unknown to anyone else. Preoccupation with land-scape and with local history has been strong up to the present time: the mark of regionalism is upon almost all our best writing. Our poetry has been above all a poetry of landscape, in which the most successful performances have usually been those that presented an exact picture, or else suggested, by musical effect, an emotion experienced in the presence of a particular scene. In poetry and prose, but more clearly in the latter, there has been a continuing attempt to describe the surface of local life with heavy stress on material environment and, in the best instances, an account of the impact of this environment on the state of mind of the pioneer or, in recent times, the resident in rural areas. Canadian writing has been in the main a supplementary kind of writing, in which the substance of most great literature was not employed. The tradition that has grown up, governing in a considerable degree even the modes and tones of expression, has not caught much that was deep in human character or very striking in thought. The few writers who have essayed something big, something central, have usually failed; and their failure has strengthened the tradition.

The tradition of Canadian poetry at the end of the First Great War was what the above account would suggest. Beginning around 1880, a movement to write about Canadian nature had been developing with a notable measure of success; one skilful craftsman had followed another, faithful to the limitations described, sharp in picture or suggestive in music, but usually weak in the passages of attempted reflection, and often in the rendering of strong emotions; this movement had passed its height by 1905, and in the following years the old themes and the old moods were reiterated to the point of becoming irksome. If a tradition had come into being, with the genuine value that a tradition always proceeds to acquire, it was a somewhat thin and narrow tradition: there was general agreement that Canadian poetry was charming and graceful, but most readers felt that it was something that could rightly be ignored in favour of other writing, English or American, that had greater interest, intensity and significance. Canadian poetry was not, it need scarcely be said, a self-contained development: romanticism and transcendentalism had marked it strongly; the milder aspects of symbolism had affected it before 1900; and later there was a superficial contact with imagism. The main forces that

were stirring in English and American poetry after 1900
had, however, but little effect in Canada: nothing of the
sharpness and firmness of Robinson and Frost had crossed
the border; nothing of the sophisticated simplicity of the
Georgians had come over from England; Pound was
someone to sneer at, Sandburg someone to laugh about.

II

Bursting out of this tight little tradition emerged the
poetry of Edwin John Pratt. Pratt was born in a Newfoundland fishing village in 1883, the son of a Methodist
clergyman. From his earliest years up to the time he was in
his twenties he was in close and natural contact with the
sea; and the influence of the sea was almost equalled by that
of the books he found in his father's library and in the small
schools to which he went in that old and poverty-stricken
colony. After some years of student preaching and elemen-
tary teaching, notably in the whaling village of Moreton
Harbour, Pratt came inland to the University of Toronto
in 1907. As an undergraduate he interested himself in
philosophy and psychology, then almost inextricably related
at Toronto, and soon after his graduation he was appointed
to lecture in the department of psychology, in which he
remained for six years. He had been ordained; and in his
choice of a theme for his doctoral dissertation his theological
interest is evident—in 1917 he presented as his thesis
Studies in Pauline Eschatology. A rather large edition
of this pedestrian argument was printed by a local
publisher; and Pratt enjoys telling how for many years
whenever he wanted to start a fire he would toss in a copy
or two of the thesis, which he refuses to list among his
publications since it was "done to a formula." Even today
in the second-hand bookshops of Toronto one comes on this
sturdy, ugly volume side by side with the slim volumes of
Pratt's verse.

In the same year appeared another book which he is just as averse to remembering. A friend undertook the private printing in New York of his Newfoundland narrative, *Rachel*, in the manner of Wordsworth's *Michael:* although in the decision to write narrative verse he was departing from the main Canadian tradition, both in the conventionality of the language and the weakness in the presentation of character the poem was stamped as imitative and ordinary. Although he was to reprint the conclusion, he now considers the whole performance unworthy and is happy that *Rachel* had no general circulation and escaped all critical notice. The writing of *Rachel* was, however, the natural result of his growing preoccupation with poetry. During the years that he was a member of the department of psychology, he was composing a good deal of verse. Soon after the appearance of *Rachel* Pratt finished a long lyrical drama, *Clay*, in which he presented a variety of philosophical systems, and towards the close introduced, to crown the whole, some ideas more or less of his own devising. One typescript of this work has survived to be the object of his own derision, and, on occasion, of the kindly amusement of his friends. He has recently described this second poetic venture as "full of theories and reflections of theories about life, ethical maxims, philosophical truisms, bald, very bald generalizations—practically the whole cargo of the department of Philosophy as it existed twenty years ago in the University of Toronto." The failure of *Clay* disenchanted Pratt with the approach to human experience by way of philosophy and psychology: it led him to seek the concrete, the intuitive, the emotional approach, it led him towards literature.

The most important opportunity of his life came in 1919 when he was invited to join the department of English in the Methodist college of the Toronto federation. The invitation to Pratt is immensely to the credit of Victoria

College. He had had no advanced training in English language or literature: he was appointed because of his creative powers, or rather because of his creative potentialities—for he had as yet published no verse of distinction beyond a few short pieces in local magazines. The college gambled on Pratt's future; and it did so because the head of the English department, Pelham Edgar, could discern in Pratt's first and groping compositions the promise of what was to come. In Pelham Edgar's small department, dominated by his fine and liberal taste, Pratt expanded at astonishing speed. Pelham Edgar, who has done more to foster Canadian literature than any other academic figure, watched his experiment with a tirelessly benignant eye. He set Pratt to lecture in the courses where he thought the material would be most valuable to Pratt's poetry. There is no doubt that the impact of Shakespeare, of Hakluyt, and of the Renaissance generally, was profound.

In 1923, four years after his appointment, Pratt brought out his first collection of poems, *A Book of Newfoundland Verse*. Many of the poems, there are about forty, reflected the local tradition; and the general effect that the book produces when read today is, that in essentials it belonged to the Canadian school then in possession. Nature is the chief theme; the predominant mood is late romantic; the experiments in verse-structure, although interesting, are never radical; there is no single strong personality shaping the whole, instead Pratt assumes a variety of points of view without much relation between any of them. Most of the pieces in the collection would be not unfairly represented by this little stanza:

> With grey upon the sea,
> And driftwood on the reef,
> With winter in the tree,
> And death within the leaf.

That is pure and right and charming; but at least four of
the elder poets then alive might have written it.   The
collection contains a few narratives, or fragments of narrative; but these are far from being the best things in it, slow
in pace, and rather ponderous in diction.   The one poem
that really pointed towards Pratt's future was a little trifle
called "The Epigrapher," in which he used the tetrameter,
exulted in polysyllables, achieved the asperity of sound
that has been one of the marks of his most characteristic
verse, and bathed the whole in genial humour.   *Newfoundland Verse* is the work of a poet who has not yet come to
grips with himself, although Pratt was forty years old when
it came out: it is the work of an experimenter who is
continuing to clutch at a tradition although that tradition
is actually stifling him.

III'

Only three years later appeared a book to which these
remarks have no application whatever.   *Titans* is the work
of a poet who has defined his personality and determined
his form.   Some of Pratt's admirers still set it above everything he has done since; and indeed it is not easy to name
any poem written in Canada at any time that is more
satisfying than "The Cachalot," the short epic with which
the book begins.   Here for the first time what is peculiar to
Pratt appeared in its full splendour; and it is pleasant to
recall that when we first read "The Cachalot," many of us
felt immediately the rare distinction of what was before us.
The other narrative which rounds out the book, "The
Great Feud," confirms the impression produced by "The
Cachalot."   A narrative of the amphibian *tyrannosaurus
rex*, who was born ages late and dominated a conflict
between the creatures of the earth and the creatures of the
sea, less dramatic than "The Cachalot," less beautifully
proportioned, it is no less satisfying in texture.

What is the originality of these poems, and especially of "The Cachalot"? It is, as the deepest aesthetic originality commonly is, the full, happy, exciting expression of an original temperament.   Pratt's choice of subject arose from his revolt against the abstract themes suggested to him by his philosophic formation; in this revolt he went back to the non-academic aspects of his experience, especially to what he had known in Newfoundland before he came to Toronto.   When he was teaching school, about 1903, he would see at Moreton's Harbour "the whaling steamers . . . tow the whales into the harbour and moor them belly up until they were taken to the factories."   He used to row out and circle about the whales, and then come back to shore and talk with the whalers.   Much of the emotion in "The Cachalot" is, in the best sense, juvenile; but the juvenile emotion combines with others to make a rich whole.

The poem immediately makes the reader think of *Moby Dick*. When he wrote it, Pratt had not read Melville's prose epic, which he was later to edit in a series for use in the schools of Ontario.   The whale, for Melville an incarnation of the evil in the universe, is for Pratt an incarnation of its strength, enviable, admirable.   In the crushing of the ship by the whale, what Pratt sees is nature imposing her strength to rend the complex contrivances of artificial society, the primitive overpowering the intellectual.   The angle from which the subject is here approached is fairly constant with Pratt: he occupied it again a decade later when he wrote *The Titanic*.   For all his admiration of the energy and gallantry of passengers and crew, his spirit was then more fully satisfied by the spectacle of the great marine machine, supposed invulnerable, destroyed by the effortless, unconscious power of the ice-berg.   The climax of *The Titanic*—it was also the passage first written, although it comes at the very end—celebrates the strength of the ice-berg:

> Silent, composed, ringed by its icy broods,
> The gray shape with the palaeolithic face
> Was still the master of the longitudes.

The originality of "The Cachalot," as of *The Titanic*, lies first, then, in the exaltation that Pratt experiences in the mere existence before his imagination of supreme strength. It is this that critics are trying to express when they call him "epic" or "heroic."

Along with his delight in strength, a violent and even a harsh quality, goes Pratt's abounding humour. The combination, or at his best the fusion, of humour and heroic strength allows him, as he has said, "to bring in with the more severe elemental qualities the human idiosyncrasies" which bulk large in his understanding of life. In the presence of strength Pratt feels pleasure as well as awe; there is very little terror in Pratt's world, and the reader never feels small in it; his pictures of strength release one from the petty round and make one feel the ally, not the victim—as with Jeffers, whom he warmly admires—of universal power. Pratt's humour removes tension, and promotes an effect of heroic ease. Simple and primitive as this humour is, it is usually expressed in terms far from epic simplicity, terms sometimes extremely erudite. He is artful in twisting the big word into a humorous effect, while caressing it at the same time for its resonant beauty. He turns even his speedy pace into something with a comic overtone: one can feel towards the end of one of the galloping passages that Pratt is getting a little out of breath and is smiling at his *tour de force*.

These and many other forms of humour are obvious in "The Cachalot." There, for the adequate projection of his strength and humour, Pratt made use of a form which has remained a favourite with him. Most of his readers speak loosely of his "tetrameter couplets," but Pratt, appreciating the danger of monotony, departs from the succession of couplets, using a fair number of quatrains, and sometimes allowing as many as ten lines to pass before a rhyme is completed. Notable versatility in the distribution of stresses further counteracts the tetrameter's penchant toward over-resonant monotony. The result of Pratt's metrical resourcefulness is admirable: "The Cachalot" abounds in energy and clamour, but it is never tiresomely reiterative. Nowhere else is Pratt's verse so conspicuously original in texture as in "The Cachalot" and its companion piece. Even in these few lines, with which "The Cachalot" opens, it is evident, I think, that Pratt has that exceedingly rare quality, absolute originality of texture:

> A thousand years now had his breed
> Established the mammalian lead;
> The founder (in cetacean lore)
> Had followed Leif to Labrador;
> The eldest-born tracked all the way
> Marco Polo to Cathay;
> A third had hounded one whole week
> The great Columbus to Bahama;
> A fourth outstripped to Mozambique
> The flying squadron of de Gama. . . .
> And when his time had come to hasten
> Forth from his deep sub-mammary basin,
> Out on the ocean tracts, his mama
> Had, in a North Saghalien gale,
> Launched him, a five-ton healthy male,
> Between Hong Kong and Yokohama.

What dash! What trumpet notes! What power of personality! This was startlingly new to our poetry, and in no other poetry is its like to be found. The nearest resemblance is with the Australian, Bernard O'Dowd, but it is distant indeed. The passage I have quoted is descriptive. But the same originality of texture is everywhere in "The Cachalot": it marks the narrative and the dialogue no less than the descriptions. What Pratt's narrative is like appears with sufficient clearness in these few lines which present a squid expecting and then enduring a grapple with the cachalot:

> Nor was there given him more than time
> From that first instinct of alarm,
> To ground himself in deeper slime,
> And raise up each enormous arm
> Above him, when, unmeasured, full
> On the revolving ramparts, broke
> The hideous rupture of a stroke
> From the forehead of the bull.
> And when they interlocked, that night—
> Cetacean and cephalopod—
> No Titan with Olympian god
> Had ever waged a fiercer fight;
> Tail and skull and teeth and maw
> Met sinew, cartilage and claw. . . .

And the dialogue is all very much like this brief interchange:

> "Two hundred barrels to a quart,"
> Gamaliel whispered to Old Wart.
>
> "A bull, by gad the biggest one
> I've ever seen," said Wart, "I'll bet'ee,
> He'll measure up a hundred ton
> And a thousand gallons of spermaceti."
>
> "Clew up your gab!"
>   "Let go that mast! . . ."

The rush and bound of the rhythm is always there, though it is not always the same kind of rush and bound. For the entire length of the poem the reader is whirled at a pace which dizzies and exhilarates him; and when the poem ends one feels that he has made a unique adventure, a journey into a realm of the imagination to which no other poet could admit him. It is notable that employing a range of

diction which so often in other poets has produced effects
which may be described as portentous or bombinating,
Pratt, throughout "The Cachalot," maintains a nervous
vigour and a fullness of meaning.   Think what such words
as "cetacean," "cephalopod," "revolving ramparts" do in
the sort of poetry where they most often occur, what a dead
weight they make and then observe, as one may in an
instant, what they add to the movement and texture of
"The Cachalot."

What happened within Pratt in the years just before
he wrote "The Cachalot"?   It was shortly before he wrote
this poem that I first met him, but my acquaintance was
wholly superficial until much later.   However, I find the
dedication to this volume of 1926 significant for anyone
who has known Pratt at any time in his mature life.   He
addresses the book to "the boys of the stag-parties."
These stag-parties of Pratt's are for many Canadians among
the best things in their lives.   They undoubtedly answer
to a deep need in Pratt's nature; and they had got under
way some little time before "The Cachalot" was written.
As I try to sum up the leading elements in Pratt I stop first
at his conviviality.   In his relations with others he is never
so much himself as when he sits at the head of his table
with half a dozen men around him, a great fowl before him,
and vigorous, easy conversation in the air.   The conversation need not be wholly or even mainly literary, but there
must be a literary temper in the language; the men need not
be intimate friends, but they must warm and soften as the
dinner goes on, so that for the moment at least they are
raised to the plane of careless friendship.   It was the host at
these parties who wrote "The Cachalot," as a year or two
before he had written for a wedding anniversary that high-
spirited, brilliant, kaleidoscopic fantasia, *The Witches'
Brew;* but in "The Cachalot" there was another Pratt, a
very secretive being who has contrived to lead an impene-

trable life behind the front of the most expansive of Canadian poets.   As a young critic wrote a few years ago:

> Pratt preferred internal planes
> Building a world so roughly grand
> He gave triumphantly the slip
> To all that ev'n Toronto planned.

A little of his secret will be seen at a later point.

IV

For about a decade the works that followed "The Cachalot" brought no significant change, if one excepts a piece of occasional poetry, the sombre and eloquent ode on his mother's death, called *The Iron Door*.   *The Titanic* has been mentioned; it was less popular and less talked of than *The Roosevelt and the Antinoe* (pronounced as if there were no terminal *e*), which tells of a rescue in mid-ocean, and is stirring and admirably managed.   Still, this poem is less deeply satisfying than *The Titanic:* in it the foreground of heroism blots out the forces of the sea which are the cause of all that occurs in it.   I do not think that Pratt intended to blot them out; I think that the drama of rescue had so many and such complicated steps that, contrary to the ideal development of the piece, Pratt concentrated upon these, and left the powerful sources of the incident to form an indeterminate back-drop.   In this tale of a rescue he comes closer to Masefield than anywhere else; and it has become the custom with some critics to think of Pratt as a local Masefield.   I do not find the comparison illuminating, and in some respects it seems to me to be dangerously mislead-ing.   Masefield's is essentially a tender nature, lacking in humour; and when he exalts strength, as he often does, there is something *maladif* in his tone as there is in Henley's or Swinburne's.   Tenderness is almost absent from Pratt's poetry: his approach to strength is much more masculine than Masefield's, and in this difference lies one of the great fundamental distinctions between the poetry of the two.

The other has to do with their treatment of character. Nothing is so difficult for a Canadian as to give a living presentment of a natural human individual. Canadian biographies never put before the reader a man in his habit as he walked and talked; they are the equivalent of marble busts. Canadian novels are full of characters who are simply the *porte-parole* of their writers, or conventionally humorous nondescripts, or pale idealizations. Only in a few short stories and novelettes, notably in those of Mr. Morley Callaghan, do real breathing individuals exist. In none of the poems mentioned up to this point could one say that Pratt made an individual live for us as Dauber lives, or Saul Kane. Pratt participates in the weaknesses of the tradition in which he grew to poetic maturity.

The closest that Pratt has ever come to animating a character with genuine life is in the latest of his major works, *Brébeuf and His Brethren*. Here he has left the sea for the Canadian past, for the most heroic achievement in our national history—the deeds of the Jesuits who came out from France in the seventeenth century and after exploits of unbelievable brilliance, and endurance as great as the type of hero-saint has ever shown, ended as martyrs. The poem centres in the figure of Jean Brébeuf; and he is as lifelike a full-length portrait as there has been in our poetry. Ten years earlier Pratt could not have drawn such a figure. He has come very slowly to believe that human beings radiate such excitement as he long found only in ice-bergs, whales, prehistoric giants and ocean storms. It will not, I hope, be mistaken for easy humour if I say that in the mould where Pratt cast his figure of the Jesuit priest something of the prehistoric giant, something of the whale, and even a little of the ice-berg remained. Brébeuf is much larger than life. A good deal is made of his physical size: he was so huge that Indians hesitated to let him into their canoes. He is always the hero; no discouragement weighs him down; no doubt divides; no horror appals; the last extremity of Iroquois torture cannot make him blench. What is fundamental to Pratt's interest in the story is suggested by his remark that he began the composition of the piece with a quest for "a simile for the Cross which would express alike shame and glory, something strongly vernacular set over against cultivated imagery and language. Two slabs of board—nails—Jewish hill, and so forth, contrasted with lilies, robes and so forth." That is not the way in which a story is begun when the chief interest is the portrayal of character: it is the way of a poet for whom character is a symbol, rather than a dramatic complex. And Brébeuf is a symbol: there is nothing complicated in him. He belongs in epic poetry, but he is not the kind of epic hero that Homer drew, or, to keep to more modest and modern names, that Morris gave us in *Sigurd the Volsung*.

In this poem the great thing is, as always with Pratt, the expression of a temperament. The temperament reflected here is quieter and graver than that which lent such fire and force to "The Cachalot." I have quoted all too little of Pratt's verse: he has never surpassed the tone and feeling that marks the conclusion of *Brébeuf and His Brethren*:

Three hundred years have passed, and the winds of God
Which blew over France are blowing once more through
        the pines
That bulwark the shores of the great Fresh Water Sea.
Over the wastes abandoned by human tread,
Where only the bittern's cry was heard at dusk;
Over the lakes where the wild ducks built their nests
The skies that had banked their fires are shining again
With the stars that guided the feet of Jogues and Brébeuf.
The years as they turned have ripened the martyrs' seed,
And the ashes of St. Ignace are glowing afresh.
The trails, having frayed the threads of the cassocks, sank

Under the mould of the centuries, under fern
And brier and fungus—there in due time to blossom
Into the highways that lead to the crest of the hill
Which havened both shepherd and flock in the days of their trial.
For out of the torch of Ragueneau's ruins the candles
Are burning today in the chancel of Sainte Marie.
The Mission sites have returned to the fold of the Order.
Near to the ground where the cross broke under the hatchet,
And went with it into the soil to come back at the turn
Of the spade with the carbon and the calcium char of the bodies,
The shrines and altars are built anew; the *Aves*
And prayers ascend, and the Holy Bread is broken.

In these lines all the clamour of "The Cachalot" is stilled:
Pratt has found for himself a grave, slow-moving, blank
verse. He will not forget this new accent. To observe the
quiet and restrained manner in which he read these lines to a
great audience in Toronto a year or so ago was to appreciate
what a change has come over him of late.

The long depression which enveloped Canada in 1929
and never really lifted until it was replaced by the worse
disaster of war was sobering to Pratt. During the 'thirties,
as a result of his growing reputation, he was giving recitals
and lectures across the country; he taught in summer
schools from Halifax to Vancouver; everywhere he went—
he is always gregarious—he saw and heard the painful facts.
Although Pratt's is not at all a political or sociological mind,
although his temperament is very unlike those of our tender
leftist poets, he was agitated by the spectacle of a society
in which scores of thousands of people had fallen into an
abyss where life was grey and numb. Disturbance in the
face of our social order runs through his little collection of
1937, *The Fable of the Goats and Other Poems*. He speaks of

The deep *malaise* in the communal heart of the world

and sees no solution for general misery. The tension in
international relations impressed him profoundly as the

'thirties drew on. In the same collection his mind can be seen following other unaccustomed paths. He foresees war. In the title-piece he attempts an allegory in a prehistoric setting, and presents his hopeful proposal for an ideal Europe. What he suggests is, in a word, that a nation should disarm its enemy by a conspicuous gesture of nonresistance. This is not one of his strongest works—Pratt's poetry is not hospitable to pure ideas, for he is still in revolt against his philosophic formation. The poem is, however, striking evidence of the change going on within him: one has only to compare it with the kindred "Great Feud" of a decade earlier to be sure of this. Elsewhere in the collection of 1937 he protests in the manner of the time against the inadequacies of brain in the leaders, whose shortcomings must be made good by the fatal courage of young heroes.

The outbreak of the war weighed heavily upon his spirit. He went back to the national past not simply, if at all, as an escape, but rather to be reassured as to the qualities of Canadian life. He wished to be sure that we could bear the strains of war. To a Canadian the lines quoted from *Brébeuf* and that poem as a whole must have a special appeal. Brébeuf and his fellow-martyrs are the Canadian types of sanctity—they are the only Canadians canonized at Rome. Theirs was a great role, perhaps the supreme role, in our heroic age—*ton histoire est une épopée*, a national anthem tells us, though we do not always believe it; nowhere are we closer to the epic level of Canadian life than when we stand on the rocky shore of the Georgian Bay where the Jesuits have built what is known as The Martyrs' Shrine on the supposed site of Brébeuf's principal mission at Sainte Marie. Pratt has often stood there: he has been "over every square foot of the ground." *Brébeuf and His Brethren* must mean more to his own people than it can to others. Consequently it is extremely difficult for a Canadian, especially so soon after the poem's appearance and before readers in other countries have recorded

their responses, to suggest what degree of universal interest
and significance the poem has.   But I do not know what
authentic poetry may be, I shall confess, if these lines, to
which a comment of Pratt already quoted refers, are not
authentic:

> Nor in the symbol of Richelieu's robes or the seals
> Of Mazarin's charters, nor in the stir of the *lilies*
> Upon the Imperial folds; nor yet in the words
> Loyola wrote on a table of lava-stone
> In the cave of Manresa—not in these the source—
> But in the sound of invisible trumpets blowing
> Around two slabs of board, right-angled, hammered
> By Roman nails and hung on a Jewish hill.

V

I have spoken almost exclusively of the narrative poet.
It is not to be forgotten that from *Newfoundland Verse*
down to the immediate present Pratt has been steadily
writing lyrical poetry as well.   If some of his lyrics are
admirable, his range in this kind of poetry is extraordinarily
limited.   Love and passion play an almost negligible part
in Pratt's poetry.   It is astonishing that in the robust
elemental world of his narratives, where his heroes and his
monstrous animals are for ever fighting and drinking and
eating, sexual desire does not exist.   When Pratt does, now
and then, speak of love in his lyrics, the note is very gentle
and the effect is weak.   He takes his place with the other
masters of Canadian poetry in shying away from the
expression of passion, and he is not in temperament
adapted, as Sangster was, or Carman, to express the pale
delicacy of immaterial love.   Nor is Pratt a nature lyrist.
Here and there, in his epic pieces, there are highly imaginative renderings of nature, passages in which nature comes
alive for a moment.   But nature is never more than the
setting for action, a background for heroes: Pratt is cordially

appreciative of Lampman and his company but the micro-
scopic is not congenial to his space- and size-loving nature.
Nor does Pratt often attempt the meditative lyric. The
best among the meditative lyrics are, I think, "Silences,"
which belongs to the collection of 1937, and "Come Away
Death," which appeared in the Canadian issue of *Poetry*,
in 1941.

The first section of "Silences" is specially impressive
and highly characteristic of the texture of Pratt's poetry:

There is no silence upon the earth or under the earth like the
    silence under the sea;
No cries announcing birth,
No sounds declaring death.
There is silence when the milt is laid on the spawn in the weeds
    and fungus of the rock-clefts;
And silence in the growth and struggle for life.
The bonitoes pounce upon the mackerel,
And are themselves caught by the barracudas,
The sharks kill the barracudas
And the great molluscs rend the sharks
And all noiselessly—
Though swift be the action and final the conflict,
The drama is silent.

There is no fury upon the earth like the fury under the sea.
For growl and cough and snarl are the tokens of spendthrifts who
    know not the ultimate economy of rage.
Moreover, the pace of the blood is too fast.
But under the waves the blood is sluggard and has the same
    temperature as that of the sea.

There is something pre-reptilian about a silent kill.

In these lines, so like the long, grave, intense verses of
Jeffers, Pratt achieves something of the quality that marks
the meditative passages in *Brébeuf*. "Silences" might
well have been an extended comment in that poem: it is not

a song, it is an intense reflection, conducted in concrete terms. Although the form of "Come Away Death" is nearer to that of song, it, too, is essentially a piece of intense reflection. The final stanzas will suggest this, as they also suggest the power Pratt has in this special kind of lyric:

> The poplars straightened to attention
> As the winds stopped to listen
> To the sound of a motor drone—
> And then the drone was still.
> We heard the tick-tock on the shelf,
> And the leak of valves in our hearts.
> A calm condensed and lidded
> As at the core of a cyclone ended breathing.
> This was the monologue of Silence
> Grave and unequivocal.
>
> What followed was a bolt
> Outside the range and target of the thunder
> And human speech curved back upon itself
> Through Druid runways and the Piltdown scarps,
> Beyond the stammers of the Java caves,
> To find its origins in hieroglyphs
> On mouths and eyes and cheeks
> Etched by a foreign stylus never used
> On the outmoded page of the Apocalypse.

Here is Pratt's lyrical power at its most impressive; and that power is obviously not that of a singing poet.

VI

It is not necessary to pass in review the other kinds of lyric that Pratt writes—the humorous lyric, the compliment, the familiar letter. None of these exhibits the remarkable force that animates the narratives and shines with a subdued glow in the best of the meditative poems.

It is the author of "The Cachalot," *Brébeuf* and *The Titanic* who rightly preoccupies us, and who has won for Pratt the central place among Canadian poets in these years.

In contemporary Canadian letters Pratt's place is unique. Some years ago I suggested that he was our only valid link between the elder and the younger poets. I did not mean that he derived from the old and produced the new. He resembles the old in some respects and the new in others and with reservations appreciates both, giving a lead to poets and critics alike to profess a generous but not spineless eclecticism. Pratt's natural generosity of taste has been strengthened by his academic studies: unlike most poets of his generation and that which followed, in Canada and elsewhere, Pratt sees great beauty in many traditions and most experiments. Whitman was not lost to him when he came to admire Eliot: Auden, from whom he has learned, has not come between him and Shelley. The breadth of Pratt's taste, along with a modest sense of his duties as a master of Canadian letters, has led him to be an active member of literary societies, a devoted Fellow of the Royal Society of Canada, and the editor of the *Canadian Poetry Magazine* from its foundation. Traditionalists and experimenters trust his judgment and work together under his high-spirited chairmanship. Pratt is also a link between the creative writers and the universities. Among writers he is always pleading for the importance of accuracy and fullness of information, of which his *Brébeuf* is a notable instance. In the universities he inveighs against the conception of a literary education which esteems a detailed knowledge of minor writers in the past more pertinent than acquaintance with the best that is written today.

His most important work since *Brébeuf and His Brethren*, a narrative of Dunkirk, has been more widely read than any other Canadian poem of merit in recent years. I have been severely reproved by a critic in the *University of Toronto Quarterly* because I did not attempt to explain the peculiar popularity of *Dunkirk* among Pratt's works, and because I did not offer an estimate of the poem. The truth is, I believe, that the popularity of the poem offers no problem: it appeared the year following the great exploit, and had it been a quite inferior performance it would have been no less popular. The subject assured the popularity of any poem written upon it, provided the poem were not enigmatic or defeatist. Nor is there any special reason for lingering over the poem here, in the attempt at an estimate. It is an admirable poem, but despite its great passages, despite lines such as

> Children of oaths and madrigals

and

> If pierced they do not feel the cut,
> And if they die, they do not suffer death

it introduces no element that is new to Pratt's art. In an essay of such dimensions as this it is not possible to pause over everything of his that is excellent. *Dunkirk*, the opera *Brébeuf and His Brethren* broadcast repeatedly over the national network of the Canadian Broadcasting Corporation, and the appearance of a collected edition of his poems in 1944 have all aided in making of Pratt a national figure. As the general public indifferent to poetry and stupidly distrustful of poets comes to know of Pratt, the place of poetry in the national society will be improved with significant though perhaps delayed repercussions on the kind of poetry that is composed in Canada.

Pratt himself popularity and respect will not alter. The essence of his genius is a deeply original thing, the expression in aesthetic terms of a quality of spirit which I have called secret, for it is something that no one but Pratt could chart, and indeed I am not sure that he could, or would chart it himself. It is perhaps too easy for those who talk with Pratt to forget that this man of unconsidered speech and homespun exuberant manner is a distinguished poet: to the unreflecting he may too often seem just one of the boys; but the reflecting know that only the outer rings of the man are penetrable, and that at the core is a secret life, the life of one who is not lonely only because he is self-sufficient.

Bibliographical Note

THERE is no wholly satisfactory history of Canadian literature or of Canadian poetry: those that are sufficiently comprehensive lack critical insight, and those with such insight are too restricted in scope. The best introductory book either for literature in general or for poetry is Archibald MacMechan's *Headwaters of Canadian Literature* (1924) which, up to 1900 at least, is admirable in perspective. The earlier period has been carefully studied by Ray Palmer Baker in his *History of English-Canadian Literature to Confederation* (1920), but readers of this excellent book need to be warned against its extreme bias toward the culture of the Maritime Provinces and away from that of Upper Canada, the modern Ontario. There is no study of comparable thoroughness on the period since Confederation; an important set of studies is W. E. Collin's *The White Savannahs* (1936), which has chapters on Lampman, Pickthall, Pratt, Kennedy, Klein, F. R. Scott, A. J. M. Smith and D. Livesay. Pre-Confederation poets are generously represented in most of the principal anthologies, among which W. D. Lighthall's *Songs of the Great Dominion* (1889), J. W. Garvin's *Canadian Poets* (second edition, revised and enlarged, 1926) and A. J. M. Smith's *The Book of Canadian Poetry* (1943) are notable. Collected or selected editions of most of the Post-Confederation poets are kept in print. The best anthology of recent poetry is Mrs. E. H. Bennett's *New Harvesting* (1938); it requires to be supplemented by *New Provinces: Poems by Several Authors* (1936), which contains poems by Finch, Kennedy, Klein, Pratt, Scott and Smith. A useful introductory anthology is Ralph Gustafson's small collection, *An Anthology of Canadian Poetry (English)* in the Pelican Library (1942).

On Lampman the best material is in the prefaces by Duncan Campbell Scott to the complete *Poems* (1900) and to the selected *Lyrics of Earth, Poems and Ballads* (1925). Lampman's lecture "Two Canadian Poets" (1891), containing important judgments on C. G. D. Roberts and G. F. Cameron, and theories about poetry and about the national society very characteristic of Lamp-

man, was edited by the present writer and published in the
University of Toronto Quarterly (1944).   There is a useful critical
biography, *Archibald Lampman, Canadian Poet of Nature* (1929),
by Carl Connor.   Miss E. M. Pomeroy has written an exhaustive
work, entitled *Sir Charles G. D. Roberts, A Biography* (1943).
James Cappon did an admirable study of Roberts for the Makers
of Canadian Literature series (1925), and a less judicial book
on Carman, *Bliss Carman* (1929); more satisfactory than this
is Odell Shepard's *Bliss Carman* (1923).   Carl F. Klinck's
Wilfred Campbell, A Study in Late Provincial Victorianism
(1942) is valuable for its fully documented account of a minor
poet belonging to the group born in the 1860's.   There is no
book on D. C. Scott; an important article is Pelham Edgar's
"Duncan Campbell Scott" in the *Dalhousie Review* (1926).
Nor is there a book on Pratt or any of the important poets more
recent than Carman and Roberts, except for J. F. Macdonald's
study of Drummond in the Makers of Canadian Literature
and Lorne Pierce's *Marjorie Pickthall: A Book of Remembrance*
(1925), which taken with the same author's brochure, *Marjorie
Pickthall: A Memorial Address* (1943), supplies the essential
information about Miss Pickthall.   On the movement since
1935 the reader may find it helpful to consult the annual surveys of Canadian Poetry contributed by the present writer to
Letters in Canada, a supplement to the April issues of the
University of Toronto Quarterly.

D. C. Scott's "Poetry and Progress" in *Transactions of the
Royal Society of Canada* (1922), Pratt's article, "Canadian Poetry
Past and Present," in the *University of Toronto Quarterly* (1938),
and A. J. M. Smith's rejoinder, "Canadian Poetry a Minority
Report," in the same review (1939), and the introduction to the
latter's *Book of Canadian Poetry*, are fundamental to an understanding of what these poets, and others, have sought to
accomplish.

CALENDAR OF SIGNIFICANT DATES

1794 Oliver Goldsmith, first native poet, born at St. Andrew's, New Brunswick
1822 Charles Sangster born at Kingston, [Ontario]
1825 Oliver Goldsmith: *The Rising Village*
1853 Charles Heavysege emigrates from England to reside at Montreal
1854 George Frederick Cameron born at New Glasgow, Nova Scotia
1856 Charles Sangster: *The St. Lawrence and the Saguenay and Other Poems*
1857 Charles Heavysege: *Saul*
1858 Isabella Valancy Crawford brought from Ireland, a child of eight, to reside at Paisley, [Ontario]
1860 Charles Sangster: *Hesperus and Other Poems and Lyrics*
      Charles George Douglas Roberts born at Douglas, near Fredericton, New Brunswick
1861 Bliss Carman born at Fredericton
      Archibald Lampman born at Morpeth, [Ontario]
1862 Duncan Campbell Scott born at Ottawa
1865 Charles Heavysege: *Jephthah's Daughter*
1867 Tom MacInnes born at Dresden, Ontario
1871 Francis Sherman born at Fredericton
1880 C. G. D. Roberts: *Orion and Other Poems*
1883 Archibald Lampman comes to Ottawa and is appointed to the Civil Service
      Edwin John Pratt born at Western Bay, Newfoundland
1884 Isabella Valancy Crawford: *Old Spookses' Pass, Malcolm's Katie and Other Poems*
1886 C. G. D. Roberts: *In Divers Tones*
1887 G. F. Cameron: *Lyrics on Freedom, Love, and Death*, edited by Charles J. Cameron
1888 Archibald Lampman: *Among the Millet*
1890 Marjorie Pickthall brought from England a child of seven, to reside at Toronto

167

168   CALENDAR OF SIGNIFICANT DATES

1893   Bliss Carman: *Low Tide on Grand Pré and Other Poems*
        C. G. D. Roberts: *Songs of the Common Day*
        Duncan Campbell Scott: *The Magic House and Other Poems*
1895   Archibald Lampman: *Lyrics of Earth*
1896   Francis Sherman: *Matins*
1897   William Henry Drummond: *The Habitant and Other French
        Canadian Poems*
1898   Duncan Campbell Scott: *Labour and the Angel*
1900   Archibald Lampman: *Poems*, edited by Duncan Campbell
        Scott
1902-4 Bliss Carman: *The Pipes of Pan*
1902   A. J. M. Smith born at Montreal
1904   Earle Birney born at Calgary, Alberta
1905   Isabella Valancy Crawford: *Collected Poems*, edited by
        J. W. Garvin
        Duncan Campbell Scott: *New World Lyrics and Ballads*
1909   Tom MacInnes: *Lonesome Bar and Other Poems*
        Abraham M. Klein born at Montreal
        Dorothy Livesay born at Winnipeg
1912   Leo Kennedy brought from England, a child of five, to
        live at Montreal
        Tom MacInnes: *Rhymes of a Rounder*
1913   Marjorie Pickthall: *The Drift of Pinions*
        Duncan Campbell Scott becomes Deputy Superintendent-
        General of Indian Affairs
1917   Marjorie Pickthall: *The Lamp of Poor Souls*
1919   C. G. D. Roberts: *New Poems*
        E. J. Pratt appointed to the Department of English,
        Victoria College, in the University of Toronto
1921   Duncan Campbell Scott: *Beauty and Life and Other Poems*
1922   Marjorie Pickthall: *The Wood-Carver's Wife and Other
        Poems*
1923   Bliss Carman: *Ballads and Lyrics*
        Tom MacInnes: *Complete Poems*
        E. J. Pratt: *A Book of Newfoundland Verse*
1926   E. J. Pratt: *Titans*
        Duncan Campbell Scott: *Poems*
1930   E. J. Pratt: *The Roosevelt and the Antinoe*
1933   Leo Kennedy: *The Shrouding*

1934   C. G. D. Roberts: *The Iceberg and Other Poems*
1935   E. J. Pratt: *The Titanic*
       Duncan Campbell Scott: *The Green Cloister: Later Poems*
1936   *New Provinces: Poems by Several Authors* (Robert Finch, Leo Kennedy, A. M. Klein, E. J. Pratt, F. R. Scott, A. J. M. Smith)
1939   Anne Marriott: *The Wind Our Enemy*
1940   A. M. Klein: *Hath Not a Jew . . .*
       E. J. Pratt: *Brébeuf and His Brethren*
1941   E. J. Pratt: *Dunkirk*
1942   Earle Birney: *David and Other Poems*
1943   Archibald Lampman: *At the Long Sault and Other New Poems*, edited by Duncan Campbell Scott and E. K. Brown
       A. J. M. Smith: *News of the Phoenix and Other Poems*
1944   Dorothy Livesay: *Day and Night*
       E. J. Pratt: *Collected Poems*

INDEX

170